WASHOE COUNTY LIBRARY

3 1235 03100 4315

S
V

NOV 2

TRADITIONAL
NATIVE
AMERICAN
BEADWORK

The Complete Guide

to

TRADITIONAL

NATIVE

AMERICAN

BEADWORK

A Definitive Study Of Authentic Tools, Materials, Techniques, And Styles

JOEL MONTURE

PROFESSOR OF TRADITIONAL ARTS
THE INSTITUTE OF AMERICAN INDIAN ARTS
SANTA FE, NEW MEXICO

PHOTOGRAPHS BY LARRY MCNEIL
PROFESSOR OF PHOTOGRAPHY
THE INSTITUTE OF AMERICAN INDIAN ARTS
SANTA FE, NEW MEXICO

Wiley Publishing, Inc.

Text and artwork Copyright © 1993 Joel Monture
Photography Copyright © 1993 Larry McNeil

Published by Wiley Publishing, Inc., New York, NY

No part of this publication may be reproduced, stored in a retrieval system or transmitted in any form or by any means, electronic, mechanical, photocopying, recording, scanning or otherwise, except as permitted under Sections 107 or 108 of the 1976 United States Copyright Act, without either the prior written permission of the Publisher, or authorization through payment of the appropriate per-copy fee to the Copyright Clearance Center, 222 Rosewood Drive, Danvers, MA 01923, (978) 750-8400, fax (978) 750-4744. Requests to the Publisher for permission should be addressed to the Legal Department, Wiley Publishing, Inc., 10475 Crosspoint Blvd., Indianapolis, IN 46256, (317) 572-3447, fax (317) 572-4447, E-mail: permcoordinator@wiley.com.

Trademarks: Wiley and the Wiley Publishing logo are trademarks or registered trademarks of Wiley Publishing, Inc., in the United States and other countries, and may not be used without written permission. All other trademarks are the property of their respective owners. Wiley Publishing, Inc., is not associated with any product or vendor mentioned in this book.

Limit of Liability/Disclaimer of Warranty: While the publisher and author have used their best efforts in preparing this book, they make no representations or warranties with respect to the accuracy or completeness of the contents of this book and specifically disclaim any implied warranties of merchantability or fitness for a particular purpose. No warranty may be created or extended by sales representatives or written sales materials. The advice and strategies contained herein may not be suitable for your situation. You should consult with a professional where appropriate. Neither the publisher nor author shall be liable for any loss of profit or any other commercial damages, including but not limited to special, incidental, consequential, or other damages.

For general information on our other products and services or to obtain technical support please contact our Customer Care Department within the U.S. at 800-762-2974, outside the U.S. at 317-572-3993 or fax 317-572-4002.

Wiley also publishes its books in a variety of electronic formats. Some content that appears in print may not be available in electronic books.

Library of Congress Cataloging-in-Publication Data:
Monture, Joel.
The complete guide to traditional native American beadwork/by Joel Monture; photographs by Larry McNeil.—1st Collier Books ed.
p.   cm.
Includes bibliographical references (p.   ).
ISBN 0-02-066430-3
1. Indians of North America—Beadwork—Handbooks, manuals, etc.
2. Beadwork—Handbooks, manuals, etc.   I. Title.
E98.B46M66   1993   93-12101   CIP
746.5—dc20

Manufactured in the United States of America.
10 9 8 7 6

Cover art:

Contemporary work, circa 1991. Two knife cases and a pictographic tobacco pouch made by Cindy Monture. (Author's collection.)

Fully beaded Lakota-style possible bag created by author and wife in 1990.

Lakota (Sioux) fully beaded moccasins, circa 1880. Classic "buffalo track" design, meaning that the green centers resemble the split-hoof tracks of buffalo, a style found in varying dark colors and proportions. These are unusual because the bordering designs on the white field are left open and airy, rather than the usual solid triangles. The tongue beading is also of a nonmatching color, and the small red area at the base of the tracks adds a certain personal touch. A yarn-dyed woven fabric, typical of pioneer women's dresses hems the tops of the moccasins. Extremely well executed, with well-defined mathematical proportions. (Courtesy of Morning Star Gallery Ltd., Santa Fe, NM.)

The author's beading board set-up, showing real and artificial sinew, threads, wax, and bead pads with a variety of traditional colors.

For my wife, Cindy, who brought three new beadworkers
into this world—Rowe:ren, Teiorakwate, and Tehotenion—and for
cousins Don Monture and Ron Monture, at Six Nations.

and . . .

to my first class of traditional beadworkers at
the Institute of American Indian Arts:
Carl, Colleen, Chester, David, Faye, Ivan, Kaoru, Kristen, Leanna, Matthew,
Michelle, Paddy, Pat, Peggy, Raelene, Ron, Ruth, Servilla, and Tommy—
All of many nations, but of one good mind.

CONTENTS

CONTENTS

ACKNOWLEDGMENTS

The author wishes to acknowledge the kind assistance and participation of numerous individuals, among them and foremost my wife, Cindy, who proofread, beaded, cooked brains, and swept out the garage; Nancy Blomberg of the Denver Art Museum, who graciously allowed me research access to the beadwork collection; Mac Grimmer and Jordan Davis, owners of the Morning Star Gallery Ltd., Santa Fe, and to staff members Robert Ashton, Joe Rivera, and Anne Abbott, who guided me through the collection and gave unsparingly of their time and advice; Paul Bullock of Attleboro, Massachusetts; Lynne Estes of Silver Hawk Gallery, Ashburnham, Massachusetts, who kept my beadwork alive during one long, cold winter; Larry McNeil, who photographed in his stocking feet; Peter Hassrick of the Buffalo Bill Historical Center, Cody, Wyoming, for permission to videotape the beadwork collection of the Plains Indian Museum for research purposes; Colleen Flores, Maudie King, and Pat White, talented hideworkers and beadworkers who demonstrated their talents herein; Lane Coulter, department head of 3-D arts, The Institute of American Indian Arts, Santa Fe, whose dedication to traditional arts helped make this book a reality; Mark Humpal, who has always supported the efforts of Native artists; Carlo, my editor, who said no, then maybe, then yes, and who is now struggling to thread a needle; and Ake'nistenha, my mother Audre, who started me beading a quarter of a century ago— our memories of you will never die.

Traditional Native American Beadwork

Introduction

A bead. A sphere of molten, colored silicate or glass, often faceted to mirror the light and glisten. Cobalt blue. Rose white-hearts. Greasy yellow. Pearl white. Crow pink. Cheyenne green. Robin's egg and pony trader. Cut brass and steel.

A single bead represents an ancient process of human decorative expression that has existed from our beginning. Beadwork is an extension of us defining ourselves, from the simple technology of a single claw or bone strung on a thong of leather, to soft stone or shell drilled with flint points, to a refined combination of intricately worked colors and patterns. A long time ago, people created meaningful icons of their existence with significant and personal objects—a tooth, a stone—and sometimes the meaning of the object lay in its difference from the ordinary, its singular beauty. It is not surprising that Native American languages have no word for *art*, because beauty exists as an element of nature and everyday existence. The very fiber of life begins with an understanding of natural gifts, an appreciation of the irrepressible forces of nature, creation, and expression. The process of stringing a bead (or a claw, tooth, or bone) reveals some connectedness to one's inner desires. It is a joyful event.

1

Creation—the building up of dissimilar parts into a unified whole—celebrates life.

The earliest North American strung decorations included stone, metal (hammered copper, silver, and gold), bones (from mammals, fish, and birds), clay, wood, and animal parts (teeth, claws, feathers, and quills). There was once a widespread trade network that moved natural products around the continent. Pacific dentalium shell was found in the Plains; maritime quahog shell was found in what are now New York and Ohio. Nations often overlapped geographically, and creative processes continually evolved, reflecting new materials and design elements, all of which are important to any discussion of Native material culture. Equally important was the shift from personal and symbolic applied arts to purely decorative applications due to influences external to Native communities—such as Caucasian rug patterns and European lace designs—or the influence of the symbolic/decorative combination on individual objects.

Beadwork does not simply exist as a technique or form. It is as evolutionary as life, because as life evolves, changes, shifts directions, so does the way we express ourselves through art. Like oral tradition, beadwork exists because of what has come before it, what shaped it, what has been "grandmothered" into it.

The grandmother of beadwork is quillwork, an intricate process of stitching (or embroidering) the dyed hollow quills of porcupine onto hide (leather) in detailed patterns. Although the porcupine has relatives (hedgehogs) in Europe and Africa, those continents never developed the embroidery art form. Quillwork is therefore unique to North America. The grandmother of quillwork is paint, originally earth ochers rubbed into hide in broad color areas or finely delineated in pictographic forms of animal relatives and sacred images.

Another aspect worth considering is that although these original forms split off in different directions, they remain—still—as family, combined. Paint, quillwork, and beadwork always reunite to compose a singular expression. Additionally, art imitates itself, such that motifs in paint or quill may be found in beadwork, from geometric to floral to pictographic. It is, in essence, that in the ancestry of Native arts, nothing exists alone; like the power of family that binds us together, so do our ways of material expression.

The evolutionary process, though, is slow, and original art forms do not die out easily, if at all. The first real beadwork might be classified as an augmentation of existing pieces or jewelry. Trade beads—those of a suitable size for necklaces or to be strung on thongs that were attached to clothing or objects previously painted or quilled—were introduced at the very beginning of European contact, probably by Cristóbal Colón. It is unlikely that any voyage from Europe—by either the Dutch, English, French, or

Spanish—failed to include a cargo a glass trade beads.

Their popularity is understandable because of the rich colors and great variety. In the fifteenth and sixteenth centuries, Venice emerged as one of the world's leading producers of glass beads, creating an astounding array of sizes and colors. The industry was controlled by families who closely guarded their "recipes" for colors. The melting and coloring of glass was an exact science, yet even today, standardized colors contain slight tonal or balance shifts in different "dye" lots. Much like dyeing yarn, each lot will not be exactly the same. Often one will see blocks of color in broad area beading from the nineteenth century. There will be significantly different color balance because the beadworker did not have enough of one color to complete the project. Matching colors is nearly impossible. Although the differences do not show up as readily in finer detail work, they can be obvious, even with white beads, on large area backgrounds.

When comparing colors, it is apparent that there was a reason these old recipes were kept secret. Modern beads, even the so-called reproductions, do not even come close to matching the deep hues and subtle shades found in the old beads. One indication of the difference is the cost; today all seed beads except for white hearts cost the same, regardless of color. Originally, because of the expense of producing a particular color, beads were priced according to the ex-

pense of manufacturing them. This is another reason why some bead colors dominate backgrounds—white or light blue, for example. Some of the early red beads—for example, a lustrous, translucent cranberry hue—contained powdered 24-karat gold in the glass to bring out the rich pigments. It might be natural to assume that red backgrounds would imitate some quillwork, but the high cost and relative supply of red beads forced beadworkers to use red as a secondary color in design elements. White as a background in broad area beading was an acceptable form that closely matched white quillwork. Interestingly enough, while black quillwork was often part of designs, black beads were not frequently used, though some examples do exist, most notably in Blackfeet or Plateau beadwork. Navy blue substituted for black in most cases by providing the strong contrasts needed to make the designs bold, even from a distance.

The methods to create a bead were actually quite simple, except in the case of multilayered or patterned trade beads. For plain seed beads, a glassblower took up a lump of molten, pigmented glass on the end of the hollow metal blowing tube and blew it up into a large thin bubble. Another man stood ready with an iron rod. Immediately—before the glass cooled —the second man stuck the rod on the opposite side of the bubble and stretched it out, creating an extremely thin strand of glass with a hollow core. The strand was broken up into short sections that were then snipped or cut up into individual beads with sharp, square edges. Thousands of beads from the same dye lot were then tumbled with hot sand or other abrasive matter until they became round, polished, and shiny. Prior to shipping to North America, Africa, or other ports of trade, the beads were strung on thread hanks of uniform size and number, then crated in wooden barrels.

Size designations for beads seem backward at first. The larger the number of the bead, the smaller the bead actually is. For instance, size 8/0 is a much larger bead than size 12/0. From smallest to largest, the current numbering of modern beads is 16/0 (extremely small and unworkable by most beaders), 14/0 (very small), 13/0 and 12/0 (a small bead used by reasonably experienced beadworkers), and 11/0 and 10/0 (used by beginners for its large size and hole). Size 8/0 is a very large bead, often called a "pony" bead because it was shipped in packs on horseback to the upper Missouri River area of the West beginning around 1820. The bead would be traded during *rendezvous* periods of the "mountain man" fur trade. A rendezvous was an annual gathering of trappers and fur traders who trafficked furs, most commonly beaver, and traded beads, blankets, and other commodities to Native Americans. As in the period before European contact, the network was extended when Native Americans distributed beads to neighboring nations.

Similarly, needle sizes correlate to bead size. A size 12 needle should be used with size 12/0 beads, though there are some instances where the hole is very tight and a needle one size smaller than the bead will ensure that the threaded eye will pass through the bead. In this case, a size 13 needle is better.

Originally, needles were not used because beadworkers were first quillworkers, and preferred the older method of embroidering with sinews and awls. Sinew, a tendon material that extends from under the shoulder blades of mammals and down either side of the spine, was cleaned of all flesh and dried. Then it was shredded into fine strands, run through the corner of the worker's mouth to dampen it, then spun under the palm of the hand across the worker's thigh to create a "thread." It was allowed to dry so the point became stiff; then the lower portion was softened in the mouth again. Holes in the hide were made with an awl, originally made from sharp bone. The stiff point of the sinew was, in effect, the needle that passed through the holes in the leather, securing down the quills or beads. Most beadwork and quillwork through the twentieth century were sinew-sewn.

Later, steel awl blades became part of the trade network. The awl blades were not round, however, because a round blade did not penetrate or exit hide as easily as a triangular blade. The triangular type was styled after military musket bayonets (military designers noted that round bayonets got stuck in a body, and found that a fluted triangle worked best). Although awl blades were not fluted after the fashion of seventeenth-century bayonets, they still performed the same function—penetrating hide smoothly.

Paralleling the rise of beadwork was the use of fabrics as a base for beadwork. The most common fabric was a tightly woven, inexpensive woolen trade cloth often referred to as *stroud* or *baize*. Usually it was dark navy blue or scarlet, but black and a deep forest green were also popular. The most economical way to create stroud cloth was to weave it naturally white, then dye it later. The two selvage edges (the sides of the cloth that were naturally bound by the weaving process) were aligned and clamped between wooden forms, and the fabric was then dipped in the dye bath. After dyeing, the wool had narrow white bands where the dye could not penetrate the fabric because of the clamping. Often, the wood forms that clamped the cloth were serrated to create a white "sawtooth" pattern running along the selvage edge. This was a popular style of cloth that the Europeans and Americans further elaborated by creating a yarn-dyed trade cloth with a rainbow selvage. Yarns were dyed before weaving, and the resulting navy blue or scarlet cloth had a multicolored selvage edge. Woolens of this sort were usually light in weight but were often used as blankets, clothing, and appliqués on hide. No examples exist of quillwork on fabric.

Next in popularity—especially among the nations of the Northeast, Great Lakes, and New England—were cotton velvets, almost always colored navy blue, wine, or purple, though green and black were sometimes used as a base for beadwork. From the fold-down flaps on soft-soled moccasins to elaborate bandolier-style shoulder bags, velvet was a significant influence in the development of eastern beadwork. Velvet also shows up in northern and Alaskan beadwork—in floral appliqué cutouts on navy blue stroud that was then edged with multi-colored beadwork.

Printed cotton calicoes were used to edge or bind leather, woolens, or velvets, and were then top-beaded with an edging technique. The early printed fabrics were generally of two colors only, no matter how small or intricate the pattern. However, given the white fabric base, the effect was of three colors. During the western reservation period (1870–1900), commodities such as flour and salt were doled out in calico sacks, which then became shirts, dresses, linings, and edge bindings.

Almost all beadwork on fabric was backed with a second cloth to cover and protect the beadwork stitches that were exposed on the back side. A common backing material was a cheap fabric called *towcloth*, a beige product woven from the unbleached fibers of flax—common linen. Even towcloth, though, was woven in surprisingly fine grades, and it is not unusual to see fine, bleached white linen used as linings or backings on early eastern beadwork.

The primary base for beadwork was and always will be hide, and the most common hide is deer—whitetail in the East, blacktail or mule in the West. It was produced by a natural method referred to today as *brain-tanned*. However, given the full range of beadwork, the various animal hides used include (in no order of importance) buffalo, elk, moose, antelope, caribou, bighorn sheep, cattle, horse, and all the furbearing mammals. (The beadwork was done on the reverse or flesh side of the hide, or applied with beaded panels or cutouts.) Certainly, the specific region dictated the primary usage. In the North, caribou or moose would prevail; in the East, deer; in the West, buffalo and elk—though these are narrow guidelines. But the place where the beadwork was done may be some indication of the type of hide used. This is an important factor in creating or understanding regional work, because the natural fauna of an area shapes and influences the work. Again, beadwork is only a component of a larger vision, and other factors contribute to a multifaceted work—feathers, fur, paint—that may be unique to a certain region. It would be unusual, for example, to see scarlet flicker feathers on a piece of Micmac beadwork from New Brunswick, except in some trade network, because scarlet flickers are western birds. But all rules are meant to be broken, and beadwork often comes

in unique and personal expressions, including the peripheral adornments.

Today most beads come from the Czech Republic, and they are generally the most uniform in size and color. Japanese beads need improvement because the holes are uneven. *Cut beads*, a term used to denote beads that have facets on them like gemstones, are more expensive, but like the old beadwork, they catch the light and sparkle so that the work radiates color.

Another type of bead that was often found in the reservation period in the West (and sometimes in floral work from the Great Lakes) was the cut or round steel or brass bead. Brand-new, the bead glistened like silver or gold; exposed to the elements, the bead took on a dark patina, a brown or green tarnish that blended into the pattern. Many steel and cut brass beads were produced in France during the nineteenth century, and they were imported to the Americas on very small hanks. They were expensive and showed up as small details in larger patterns. A variation on the cut metal bead was a brass, bronze, or steel bead with diagonal lines repeating around it, such that the effect of the beads stacked against each other was that of a twisted rope. Other unusual beads that occasionally show up are copper and bronze—sometimes cut, but most often polished and round. Glass and metal are both earth elements, and their combination in beadwork is not only very natural but pleasing. Glass typically is thought of as fragile, and metal as permanent and strong; thus there is a unique balance in their combination. Yet it is not unbalanced, because the use of metal beads is not excessive. Rather, it is more like a garnish to add sparkle and a teasing sense in the finished piece.

Though not strictly a beadwork technique, but within the metal category of sewn decorative art, sequins must be included. The early sequins were made of loops of silver, brass, or copper that were stamped or flattened under pressure to produce a disc with a hole in the center. Original sequins will display a "seam" running from the middle to the outside edge, and often a tiny indentation at the outer line of the seam. Sequins were most often used on fabric, including woolen dresses and breech cloths, vests, and bustle trailers, but they occasionally show up as trim on hide work. Sequin work in combination with beadwork is a vibrant addition, and like cut metal beads, it mellows with the patina of age to "relax" into the finished piece. In silver, a sequin is like a full winter moon casting a glow across a landscape of beads; in brass, the sequin reminds one of the harvest moon climbing high in the October night above the cornfields. Sometimes, an orange moon comes up so large and so important that a single copper sequin seems the perfect and simple expression.

HIDES

It cannot be overemphasized how important the hide or leather is upon which the beads are sewn. Commercially tanned leather is the most common type used today, and it is the least expensive, with deer or elk readily available from $2.50 to $4.50 per square foot. An average deer hide measures between 8 and 12 square feet, with elk around 15 to 20. All commercial hides are run through a machine with rollers that measure every square inch, including missing hide in holes. The hides are hand-marked with a size in red, white, or black pencil, usually on the edge of the flesh side near a hind leg. The markings denote fractions of square feet—for example 22/3 or 9/1. The first number represents the entire square footage, and the second number (not always divided by a line, but instead appearing as a raised numeral) denotes the fractions: 1 means one-quarter, 2 means one-half, and 3 means three-quarters. Thus, 22/3 means 22¾ square feet. But every part, including thin leg strips, is measured; animals don't come square, and neither do hides.

Commercial hides are usually split or shaved to be uniform in thickness, but often the necks or spines will be considerably thicker than the belly edges. As a hide gets cut up for smaller objects, it becomes unpredictable where the next pattern will be cut, and for this reason choosing hides with a fairly uniform thickness will ensure a better finished product.

However, there are several problems with commercial leather. First, the chemicals and heavy salts used to tan the skin are not only degrading to the environment, but they produce a hide robbed of its natural oils—dry and impermanent. A comparison between commercial leather and Native tanned hide will demonstrate just from the added chemicals a product that is twice as heavy and dense as Native leather. This makes it weightier and less desirable for clothing and beadwork, which itself can be very heavy. Eventually, chemicals break down the structure of the fibers, and this process weakens or destroys the threads of the beadwork. A pair of boots in the attic will become thumbnail brittle, but Native leather will remain for centuries as supple as it was the day it was made—barring exposure to moisture. Moisture and water are great destructive forces on leather, commercial or otherwise. Though not a problem for leather tanned with the hair off, another situation can occur with hair-on *robes*, which are the skins of buffalo or elk. When a robe is used on the ground, the moisture (and/or earth elements in the moisture) causes a natural glue in the hide to emerge from the skin. The surface of the hide looks like mucilage had been applied, and the hide can literally crack and break. Deer and moose hides are almost

worthless with the hair left on, because the hollow, brittle hair breaks off easily and gets all over everything.

A second problem is one of esthetics and traditional respect for the animals. The hair is "slipped" with chemicals or harsh lyes in the commercial process so that the hair slips out of the follicle, leaving the upper epidermal layer of the skin intact. This is why commercial leather is smooth on one side (the hair side) and rough like suede on the flesh side (the side against the animal). Beadwork done on commercial leather must be on the rough, or flesh, side, which means that the actual work is on the inside of the animal, an unnatural notion to Native people.

All Native beadwork, or any applied embroidery such as quillwork, was done on the grained outside—the natural side—of the animal so that garments were worn the way the animal wore its hide: flesh side in, hair side out. This way respected both nature and the animal. Sometimes people try to use commercial hide this way, but the upper epidermis, smooth and polished, does not look proper. Nor will the hide be strong enough for some beadwork techniques.

In support of this theory of respect for the hide's inside and outside, it should be noted that it was often common for Plains peoples to use the cutoff tops of cavalry boots for knife cases or ration coupon pouches, and in all instances the beadwork was done on the hair side, which was polished, smooth scarf skin. It should be noted too, that commercial leather was always used out of necessity rather than by choice, since Native people had been deprived of natural resources to make their own leather. This was especially true among Plains peoples who were forced onto reservations. When cattle were brought in and distributed by the Indian Agent responsible for beef rations, the hides were treated exactly like buffalo or elk, and tanned the right way. Such cattle included horse, sheep, or goats.

The only time beadwork was done on the flesh side—and it often was—was on the tanned hair-on robes of buffalo or elk. This was true of quillwork also. Beaded or quilled stripes in matching parallel rows, or in a wide band with rosettes, often covered a seam, because large robes were frequently split in two down the spine and tanned in two pieces because of the unwieldy size. Then the finished tanned robe would be finely stitched together and the seam covered over with beadwork. Blankets were similarly beaded but always upon a band of hide, which was then sewn on later. One reasoning behind this was that by the time a robe wore out (which took considerable time), the beadwork might not be in such good shape. But blankets wore out quickly, and the beaded band would simply be transferred to a new blanket. Thus, it is interesting to note that the unique art of beaded blanket bands evolved from the tanning procedure of splitting large hides.

There is also a modern hide on the market sometimes referred to as *Kootenai* skin, which is hand-worked to be rough on both sides like Native-tanned hide, but chemically tanned and machine softened. It is an imitation that is also very unstable with moisture and time. It is also dense like commercial hide, and heavy, lacking the light, fluffy texture of brain-tanned hide. Kootenai hide is generally made from deer or antelope. Both Kootenai and commercial leathers are tougher to bead upon, because of the tight fiber structures created by the chemical process. Still, they do provide for extremely tight beadwork on small objects.

Even though most people were forced to put away the hide tools for the shovel and the hoe, some continued tanning hides the original way into the twentieth century. These are people to whom we are grateful, because today the old ways of tanning hides are still with us, and growing! From James Bay to Alaska to Montana and Arizona, Native people continue to make leather. Although the principles are the same, there are different ways—all of them 100 percent natural. This kind of leather satisfies not only the individual and the community, and it continues like generations to grow and expand. So often the old hideworking tools lie dormant on museum shelves or in private collections, sadly alone. There is an energy in the old tools because the people who made and used them did so with care and love, making the skins needed to clothe families and to do quill and beadwork on. There is also the knowledge that the process is safe, without residue or chemicals. Fortunately, new tools are being made, and so are the skins for beadwork.

One way to think about hide is to imagine a cotton ball, a mass of fibers held together with glue. This is what rawhide is like—hard and stiff like sheet metal—but in tanned hides the fibers are softened, the glue neutralized, the skin dry and fluffy, smooth like velvet. In commercial tanning the fibers are impregnated with chemicals, the hide put through rollers, tumbled, softened, and the overall effect is a dense, heavy mass much like the felt in a cowboy hat.

In Native tanning, the fibers and glue are broken down or neutralized with enzymes or oils. Some Native peoples use the brains of the animal—hence the term *brain-tanned*—and it is said that each animal has exactly enough brains to tan its own skin. Those peoples around James Bay use fish or bear oil, but bear oil is preferred. In Alaska, some people use a combination of red willow bark and clay, with the bark containing a natural tannic acid. Hopi women are known to chew squash or pumpkin seeds and rub the oils into the skin as they stretch it in a conversation circle. In the Yukon, brains are used. Other Native peoples use raw eggs mashed with melted fat. The point is to penetrate the skin with some agent that counteracts the glue to make those fibers come apart. The hide becomes open, spongy, and light in weight,

which also makes it more "breathable," more comfortable to wear against the skin, and more able to naturally fit the contours of the body. Beadwork tends to "set" deep into Native hide, which melds it together, but on commercial hide the beads ride a little higher, making the work more prone to damage.

Needles and awls pass easier through Native hide, but in commercial hides the holes "cut" through the leather and remain more open, creating a looser, less stable beadwork. The overall effect of beading on Native hide is a flatter, more integral melding of materials. This is also true of seams, especially those sewn with natural materials such as sinew. The seams on Native hide pieces may be flattened with a polished antler or horn tool in order to lie perfectly flat—ideal for beading over—but commercial seams still remain slightly ridged, which can show up later in the beadwork.

ABOUT NATIVE HIDEWORKING

There are two myths about Native leather: The first is that brain-tanned hide will dry out like rawhide if it gets wet. The second is that smoked hide is waterproof. Neither claim is true. Wet brain-tan will stiffen significantly, but it will soften easily and with use—for example, with a pouch or a pair of moccasins. However, wetting brain-tan may stretch it out of shape and distort the beadwork sewn upon it.

Smoke-tanned hide (actually a misnomer, since the hide is smoked in a thick smudge of sweet smoke until it becomes a light honey to dark brown color *after being tanned with brains, or fish or bear oil*) is not at all waterproof. The creosote or resins in the smoke "soak" into the fibers of the hide and help protect it from damage due to wetting, but the hide is still porous and water will pass through it and any sewn seams. A smoked hide, such as moose tanned with oils, may be a little more resistant to water when new, but as the oils dry out, the hide is no more waterproof than any other piece of leather.

For the purposes of this discussion, we will focus on deerskin, the most common Native-tanned hide. But all large leather mammals—buffalo, moose, elk, antelope, bighorn sheep—could be substituted. With the exception of removing the hair, all furbearers (beaver, otter, etc.) and robes (buffalo, elk) can be worked with these methods.

Foremost to consider is the initial treatment of and respect for the hides. The original peoples gave thanks for all parts of the animal and respected all parts equally, not just the meat, as modern hunters do. To be disrespectful, or to waste, was to risk having bad luck. Animals then would not come to you, because the belief is that animals give themselves only to respectful hunters. Properly treated, the animal is divided among the people, while some are butchering the meat, others are taking care of the hide and other parts. It's wrong to toss the hide aside and ignore it until later. Sometimes things happen and the hide goes bad because we become too busy. This is disrespectful. A hide clothes us, protects us, and is regarded as an intimate shelter. A hide is no different from meat left out to spoil, and it will spoil quickly if not cared for properly. All proteinaceous material in the raw state contains moisture and bacteria that, combined with warmth, will begin the process of decay. The only way to avoid this, short of freezing, is to remove those elements that cause the problem. The old-timers knew this, and took care of it immediately.

European methods included salting raw ("green") hides to temporarily preserve them. Salt is a chemical that leeches moisture and oils out of a hide. It may be fine to use salt if the hides are to be chemically tanned in a factory, but it is unsuitable for natural Native tanning. Salt is a pickling agent, acidic and harsh. A salted hide that is subsequently fleshed, stretched, and dried will exhibit a white crystalline pattern on the surface, like winter frost on a windowpane. Salt is also a mineral, and the metal blades of scraping tools will be continually dulled working a surface impregnated with salt, much like honing the edge of a knife on a whetstone.

For those who are interested in learning more about tanning hides naturally, the Native American way, see Appendix 2: Native American Hide Tanning, for how-to instructions for naturally preparing a hide yourself. For those who are buying commercially tanned products, you're ready to move on.

GETTING STARTED

Good work habits will help the beadworker stay organized and produce faster results. The following methods are considered the most efficient by many experienced beadworkers.

First, cut a beadwork pad about 6 inches by 6 inches square out of a piece of medium-weight leather. One technique is to use a light-colored leather pad for dark beads such as reds, navy blues, or greens, and a dark or black piece of leather for the light beads, whites, yellows, and pinks. So often one sees a beadworker with a bowl of loose beads or a jar lid filled with beads. Unfortunately, the beads roll around when you try picking them up with a needle, and the process becomes much more time-consuming. By using bead pads, you may speed up your work by being able to cull out beads to the side that are misshapen or have imperfect holes, plus the beads are not skipping around. There is the added advantage of being able to place little piles of all the colors you are working with on one pad, thus eliminating the time and trouble of reaching around to a variety of bowls or jar lids, and taking aim again. Laying the edge of your hand down, you may then use the needle like a dart, directing it to the color of bead you will use next.

Next, cut a piece of 1-by-12-inch clear pine approximately 16 inches long. Sand down all rough edges and corners and rub with linseed oil. You may also decorate the top of the board near the outside edges with brass tacks or rub red ocher or other paint onto it, as was done to tobacco cutting boards. The great advantage of this is that your bead pad (with all the colors on it) and all of your other equipment and supplies may be placed on the board. You may then do your beadwork with the board on your lap, at a table, or sitting in the grass. You could even do beadwork riding in a car on the way to a powwow. The board is a portable work center, which may be put on a high shelf away from children (or cats). It is inexpensive, easy, organized, and efficient.

Next, consider adding to your kit a pair of small, 5-inch Fiskars scissors (the orange-handled variety) with a *sharp*, not rounded, point. The sharp point often allows you to get between rows of beads or under your beadwork to snip thread ends. And the Fiskars company produces a sharpener that fits your scissors. Like all tools, they need to be kept in a good, sharp condition.

Another necessity is a good awl, maybe even two—one large and one small. The blade should be filed into a triangular shape with a slow, gentle taper, such that using only the tip of the blade will result in a small hole, and running the awl to the base of the blade will produce a larger hole (Figure 1). The handle should not be a large, bulky object, but rather delicate. Wood or antler was a very common material for awl handles, but the penis bone of otters or bears is also used for awl handles, though such handles are not easy to find these days. A longer, slender handle was most common, not the knobby type of handle used on modern carpenter scratch awls; this is supported by the thousands of extant beaded awl cases that are all long, tapering tubes, like a carrot. Handle sizes should be the same, so that the awl case might be used for either the big awl or the small one—the only difference being in the relative thickness of the blade. A hardened masonry nail may be ground down on a *cool* grinding wheel, being careful not to get it so hot as to lose its temper. An appropriate-sized hole is drilled in the base of the handle and the blade inserted, either by being driven in to provide a friction fit, or bonded in place with epoxy. The blade should be kept sharp on a fine stone, such as a white Arkansas whetstone, using light oil on the stone.

It is now necessary to gather needles, thread, beeswax, beads, hide (leather) or cloth.*

English-made beading needles are most commonly available, and are essentially sharpened wires with a long, oval eye. The size of the needle should

---

* A list of sources for materials, revised at publishing date, is provided in the appendixes.

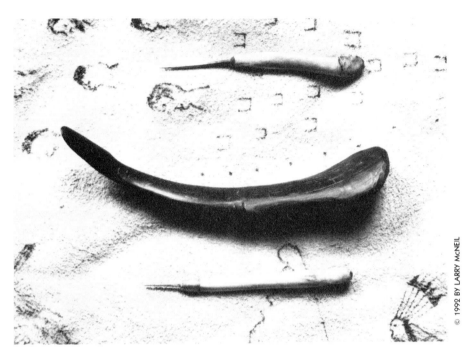

FIGURE 1 · Old-time sewing tools: Two awls with diamond-shaped steel blades set in an otter penis bone (*top*) and a bear penis bone (*bottom*). A carved, polished buffalo horn quill flattener also used to burnish sewn seams (*middle*). (Author's collection.)

FIGURE 2 · On the main body of the bag, Maudie King, Iroquois, demonstrates how the needle goes straight through the hide, not coming down and at it from an angle. This helps prevent very bent needles or needle breakage. On this piece, a running Iroquois "sky dome" pattern traverses the border of the bag.

correspond to the selected bead size—for instance, a size 12/0 bead would normally require a size 12 needle, though sometimes the bead hole might be smaller, requiring a size 13 needle. It is a wise idea to have a needle that is one size smaller than the beads in use in case that problem occurs. Remember that just as in beads, the larger the number, the smaller the needle. The needles on today's market are numbers 10, 11, 12, 13, 14, and 15, the latter being so small as to be like monofilament. English needles come in small, black paper packages of twenty-five count, and are very inexpensive. They are like tempered wire or spring steel and have a lot of play, but will break if bent to extreme angles. The most experienced beadworkers master the art of positioning the needles against the work so that the needle pierces straight through the hide or cloth, not entering at an angle and having to bend the needle to complete the stitch. Needles are available in long or short lengths—the choice depends on the beadworker.

An unthreaded needle will easily pass through all beads of the same size as the needle, and often even smaller beads. However, the added bulk or thickness of the thread passing through the eye is where problems occur. Thus, the selection of thread is important. There are three kinds of sewing material: Sinew, an animal product, does not require needles but an awl, which first makes the hole, the dry tip of the sinew serving as the

"needle" that passes through the hide (Figure 2).

Cotton or linen thread was used in the old days when needles became available, and it added to the convenience because sinew threads are short and need to be knotted off and started again. Spun threads allowed the beader to work much longer without interruption. The best modern thread is a size 50, standard cotton/polyester-core sewing thread, but here's a tip! Instead of using standard white, use a thread color that matches your hide or cloth—perhaps a beige or pale brown. No beadwork is perfect, and it is not unusual for threads to be visible on close examination. A thread that is the color of the hide will take on an almost chameleon-like effect, blending into the work rather than glaring like a white thread would!

A size 50 thread will fit through most needles, though with greater difficulty when you work with one smaller than size 13. Threading a beading needle is one of life's frustrations for the beginner, and the easiest way is to make sure the end of the thread is cut off straight across, with no loose fibers to impede your progress through the needle. The eye of the beading needle is a narrow elongated oval and the thread is a circle wider than the oval. Wet the end of the thread in your mouth and flatten it by drawing it between your thumb and forefinger with the needle against the thread. Or put the thread on the work board and hold your needle against it as you draw the thread out. In short, the thread must fit through the eye, and since the eye won't change, the thread must. The flat side of the thread is then aligned with the elongation of the needle's eye, and with steady hands the needle is threaded!

Cotton/polyester thread is quite strong and durable, and it has as much tension as sinew (tension meaning the ability to lock the stitch down as tight as it needs to be). But it is not always possible to use cotton/polyester thread in the smaller beads 14/0 or 16/0. These are the bead sizes that usually only more advanced workers use, and the thread marketed today for use in smaller needles is called *Nymo*, a nylon product. Size 00 is most commonly used. However, Nymo has a great amount of spring or stretch to it, and the stitches must be uniformly tightened to ensure even tension.

Other beadworkers have used monofilament fishing line and even dental floss, which can be split down into smaller sizes, but these are not recommended.

Beeswax is used to coat the threads before sewing, and it is a simple process. Pull about four feet of thread off your spool (about two arm's lengths will do) and thread the needle, gently pulling the thread through the eye to the middle point in the length of the thread. When you hold up the needle, the two loose ends of the thread should match.

Now the thread will be waxed with a small cake of beeswax, available in one-ounce sizes about as big as a silver dollar and about one inch thick. Holding the needle, lay the thread against the cake of beeswax and pull it across the wax as though you were trying to saw through it, which in effect you would do if you held it in the same groove every time. The thread will become coated with wax, and the two lines will stick together. Make sure the two threads *are* together, because the point is to have a single beading thread composed of two lines fused together. The purpose of this is to prevent tangling and to keep the thread from moving back and forth through the eye of the needle as you sew, which would fray and break the thread! The needle and the thread must become one unit, and as you bead and the wax wears off, you should rewax the thread. There are other advantages in that the wax protects the thread from moisture over time; it also adds bulk to fill the hole in the beads, making for tighter and stronger beadwork, though this is somewhat negligible. Both cotton and Nymo threads should be waxed, but never wax sinew, which is simply moistened in the mouth while beading.

Although size 10/0 beads are the easiest for beginners to work, they pose very little challenge, and the patterns created with them are not as finely wrought. Size 11/0 beads enable the worker to create slightly finer designs and work on smaller objects, and it is a good medium size for the beginner to use. Color choice is not as important as color usage from an aesthetic standpoint. Just as there is poorly conceived art, the same is true of beadwork, even though the techniques may be very good. Color and pattern are the compensating factors for a technique that is slightly inexperienced. A harmonious blending or contrasting of colors is essential in good traditional beadwork, and the softer, though not necessarily dull, colors merged in sharply contrasting patterns almost always result in good beadwork, creatively speaking. The finest beadworkers, whether in Lakota geometric style or Ojibwe floral style, choose colors that are compatible and then strive to create contrasts so that no colors become lost or secondary in the work. It is striking how even with soft or muted colors, each one will stand out from the work, sometimes at a considerable distance from the viewer.

However, it should be remembered that the color of the hide will affect the overall appearance of the beadwork. Even more important is to realize that over time the hide will darken, further affecting the look of the work. It is interesting to note that many believe that white or natural hide was used for ceremonial dress, and that everyday clothing or objects were always made from smoked hide. This does not seem to bear out, for 90 percent of extant objects are beaded on plain hide, from tipi bags to saddlebags, knife cases, awl cases, leggings, moccasins, etc. Smoked hide, traditionally moose and caribou, seems to have found its niche in the twentieth century, having been brought down from the North either whole or in moccasins, gloves, bags, and other objects for the commercial market. The true smoked hide had its origins in snowy and subarctic regions where moisture was a consideration, and the fact that the hides are tanned with fish or bear oil indicates a technology influenced by climatic conditions. The oils permeated the fibers in the hide and protected it against water more than the smoking process did.

White hides that were favored for special-occasion wear or ceremonial use were cleaned by rubbing with white clay, much like the early British army used white china kaolin balls to rub on uniform cross-belts and gaiters. The clay did not so much clean as cover stains or dirt, yet it may also have provided some protection against future scuffs. But smoking hides was and is very common, and today beadwork done on smoked hides generally commands a higher price. It is recommended that the beginning beadworker start out properly by using only Native tanned hide, both for reasons of esthetics and ease of stitching.

ABOUT BEAD COLORS

Note: Beads are manufactured from opaque glass or from a translucent or transparent colored glass like that found in bottles.

WHITE   This is by far the most commonly used color, both in eastern-style edging and floral or curvilinear art, and in western solid area backgrounds. Beadworkers should generally have two or three times as much white as any other color, with perhaps one exception: blue.

BLUE   Medium blue is the second most commonly used background color. However, the five blues that should be used are: (1) a very dark opaque navy blue; (2) a very dark transparent (translucent) navy blue; (3) a medium blue, often called bluette (or a medium translucent blue, often called pony trader blue today); (4) a light blue of an almost turquoise hue; and lastly (5) a pale sky blue, almost washed out.

GREEN   A dark green, almost like foliage, in both opaque and transparent varieties; a medium opaque green, often called Sioux green; and a paler but not too light opaque shade, sometimes referred to as apple green, are standards in traditional beadwork.

YELLOW The old yellows were so rich as to have a deep, buttery quality, hence today they are referred to as "greasy yellow." Unfortunately, there is no bead on the market today that compares to the old secret family recipes. The same holds true for the greasy oranges, which had a deep pumpkin coloration. The yellows on the market today seem too bright and gaudy, almost neon. There are currently greasy yellow reproductions, and these are recommended above all other yellows, but they have a slightly muddy quality about them. However, this situation does have one positive effect: Use of these greasy yellows is a sure sign to collectors or museums that the piece is a forgery! There is also a pumpkin yellow being produced that is an opaque bead with a fairly rich hue in between yellow and orange, and a nice bead. A medium transparent golden yellow is also a good choice.

RED The most beautiful old color may have been the white heart! This was a bead with an opaque white core covered with a golden red transparent outer layer that glistened. Sometimes it was a soft, gentle rose color in appearance, and was called rose white-lined. Other times it had a dark cranberry effect. Regardless, it was always stunning, even in its subtlety. Today the white hearts are being produced again and they are usually quite nice, but they are generally twice as expensive as standard one-color beads. A plain opaque red bead was seldom used, though every rule has its exception. Instead, a transparent deep cranberry-like bead was substituted for the white-heart variety, and it is also available today.

PINK Most frequently called Crow pink because of that nation's skillful and wonderful use of it in broad area beading, it had a "greasy" quality to it like the yellow, and almost overtones of blue or purple. It was and is ideal with pale blues and yellows divided by white or navy for contrast. Some of the vibrant pinks on the market are not colorfast, and seem to fade after time. Try to find and use only reproduction Crow pink, which some dealers for unknown reasons are calling Cheyenne pink.

BLACK Black was very infrequently used, and is not recommended for beginners because it is so overpowering that it detracts from the other bead colors.

OTHER COLORS Notwithstanding the "all rules are meant to be broken" clause, other colors such as the ranges of purples, oranges, etc., are fairly modern in usage and popularity, and do not belong in traditional beadwork. Worthy of mention again, however, are the delightful metal beads—steel, brass, and copper, both in rope twist and cut with facets. They are not made today with nearly the same craftsmanship or beauty, but they definitely deserve consideration and should be used frequently, if sparingly.

Lastly, many of the above bead colors are available in the "cut" variety—with facets like the metal beads—and these deserve attention. Cut beads add sparkle and excitement to a work of art, especially when used in small detail areas of a larger piece or in floral patterns.

When buying beads, it is best to buy in bulk—at least half a kilo at a time—to ensure uniformity of size and color, especially taking into consideration the amount of beads needed to complete the work. A hank of beads is about ten inches long and composed of twenty-four strands of threaded bead. Sewn in solid beadwork such as a lazy stitch, one hank will cover approximately 17.5 square inches or an area about 3 by 6 inches. A half-kilo of beads contains approximately fifteen hanks and will cover an area of about 260 square inches, or, for instance, 12 by 21 inches. These are the approximations for size 12/0 beads, though the other sizes are comparable. There are more beads per kilo in the smaller size, less in the larger sizes, but proportionally the same area is covered.

Note: Many mail-order suppliers will furnish customers, for a small fee, with a chart of real beads for color and size comparison. Ask for this service.

═══ BEADWORKER'S CHECKLIST ═══

Beading board
Beeswax
Size 11/0 beads

Leather pads
Size 11 needles
Brain-tanned deer hide

Scissors
Size 50 thread
Awl

Traditionally, women were beadworkers (though today some of the best new beadworkers are men). They kept their tools with them wherever they went, usually hanging from their belts, especially in Plains cultures. A woman's belt set consisted of a beaded pouch containing sinew threads or threads and needles, a beaded awl case with awl, and a beaded knife case or sheath. The beadwork almost always matched on belt sets and also served as an example of the worker's skill and artistry. There were quillworker and beadworker societies composed of the most industrious and talented artists, which essentially served to teach others and provide examples for the community to follow. It is not uncommon to see miniature moccasins or other miniature objects that were made in the spirit of contest by the members of the society to celebrate their work. Often

FIGURE 3 · Hotinonshonni (Iroquois) beadworker Maudie King using a lap board and a black leather pad to demonstrate how the white beads stand out as the needle passes parallel over the beads, picking them up easily. Maudie rests one hand on the board, with the needle close to the beads. She holds the work in her other hand, keeping the thread draped away to prevent tangling.

FIGURE 4 · Omaha beadworker Colleen Flores with a work board and a light-colored bead pad doing lazy stitch on a scissors case. Her design is made up of red, navy, and yellow on a pink background.

contests were held in which women displayed their work for the pride of their families and communities. Among the Lakota, a quilled or beaded cradleboard was considered the crowning achievement.

A young woman's first menses was considered the time for her to put away childish thoughts and turn her mind toward becoming industrious. Her mother would spend four days teaching her all she needed to know about beadwork (or quillwork), and the first things a girl would make would be the awl case, belt pouch, and knife case for the tools that would allow her to be an industrious woman. For four days all she would do was bead or quill, for it was believed that if she didn't, she would be a lazy person.

With this in mind for the beginning beadworker (or a beadworker with experience who is branching out), the next section will go through the creation of a beadworker's belt set . . . the traditional way!

= The BEADWORKER'S BELT SET =

The Basic Stitches: The Whip Stitch
᭝᭝᭝᭝᭝ and the Running Stitch ᭝᭝᭝᭝᭝

The pouch or bag is where all the necessary small supplies are kept—thread or sinews, beeswax, needles, small scissors, etc. There are several styles and many interesting variations, but the most common are the plain square, flapped pouch with an unfringed T seam, or the small round or oval fringed pouch. The size and dimensions are subjective, but Figure 5 provides basic guidelines. A variety of stitching techniques for leather construction are illustrated in Figure 6. The basic "whip stitch" and the basic "running stitch" are used in almost 100 percent of Native hide sewing. Remember also that when using brain-tanned hide, they are sewn up inside out with the flesh side showing, then turned so that the hair side is the outside.

There are three ways in which the pouch may be sewn: The first is with natural sinew rolled into a thread with the tip dry, and functioning as the needle and passing through the hole pierced close to the edge with your awl. The second way is with a size 10 beading needle, threaded with waxed size 50 thread. The third is with a single strand of artificial sinew; it comes on a large spool and can be split down

FIGURE 5 · BELT POUCH PATTERNS

ONE-PIECE POUCH

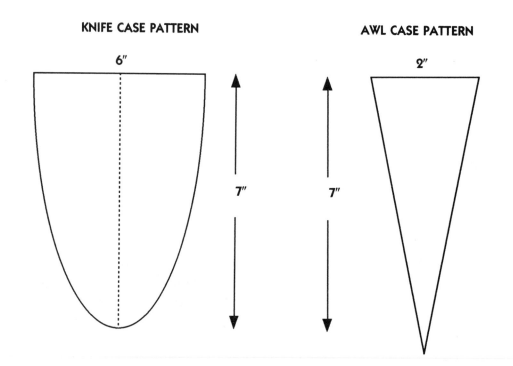

TWO-PIECE POUCH

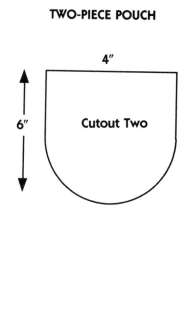

FIGURE 6

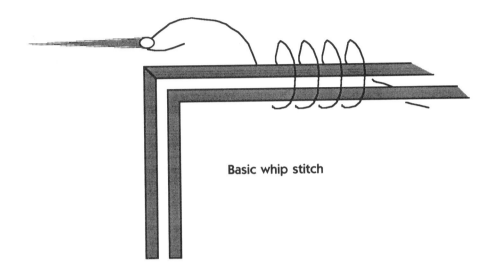

Basic whip stitch

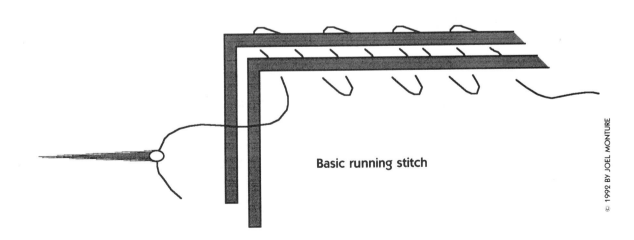

Basic running stitch

© 1992 BY JOEL MONTURE

to the desired thickness for use in a saddler's, glover's, or blunt tapestry style needle, which passes through the awl holes. For both pouch styles, the whip stitch is used, and rather than knotting the thread, leave about an inch hanging out when you start and sew over it so it becomes integral to the seam. It cannot pull out and is the old way of sewing with natural sinew. To end your stitching, simply sew back through two or three holes and bring the last stitch through itself, locking it down tight, then clip off the remaining thread. When sewing with sinew, as it begins to run out and a new thread is needed, continue sewing with the new sinew over the ends of both the old and new thread, thereby locking down the old and new ones without using knots.

Beginning beadworkers and hideworkers are encouraged to create paper patterns, though with experience many projects can be "eyeballed," meaning that as confidence develops patterns are not always necessary. The pattern can be outlined using a soft pencil or pen, but the leather project should be cut out inside the lines so that there are no marks on the leather. Another method is to "score" the outline with the tip of the awl or scissors, but the lines can disappear into the hide as it is handled. Save patterns for standard projects.

The square (or rectangular) pouch is the basic design also employed in larger tipi bags, saddlebags, and other containers that are not envelopes with flat bottom corners, but expanded with a square profile (Figure 7). The side seams are sewn up from the bottom to the top, and then the bottom is brought up and sewn across in a T-shape final seam. As in all sewing, especially if there is to be beadwork over or covering the seam, the seam should be flattened on the inside with a flattening tool made of polished buffalo horn, antler, or bone. This will press the stitches down into the hide and "burnish" the sewing. All of these steps are necessary considerations in creating beadwork with traditional qualities. Beadwork does not so much stand alone, but rather is a part of a larger composition in which each detail combines to unify the work. Sloppiness in any part detracts from the unified whole.

When the small square pouch is turned out, a tie thong is run through holes in the outside corners of the top flap, pouch front, and pouch back, which can then be tied in loops to hang from the belt. Two holes are pierced with an awl (not cut with a knife of scissors) on the pouch flap, equidistant from the ends, and holes are pierced in the pouch front for tie thongs to secure the bag closed. Now it is ready for beading.

The second pouch style—round with a square top—is composed of a front and back piece, plus a strip of hide anywhere from 2 to 4 inches (or more, depending on personal taste), which serves as the fringe. The fringe piece is inserted between the front and back, with the fringe to be cut *inside* the bag. The three pieces are tightly

FIGURE 7

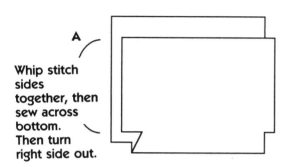

A

Whip stitch sides together, then sew across bottom. Then turn right side out.

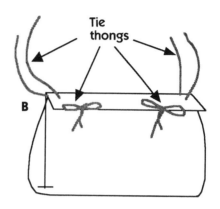

Tie thongs

B

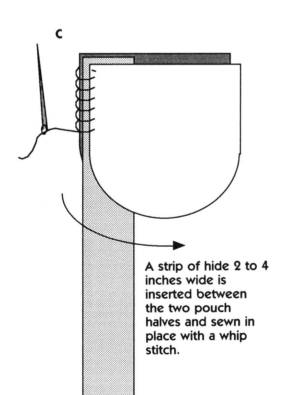

C

A strip of hide 2 to 4 inches wide is inserted between the two pouch halves and sewn in place with a whip stitch.

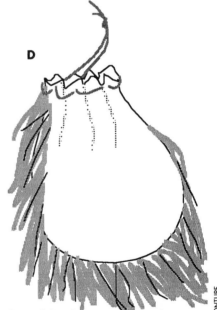

D

Turn right side out, and cut narrow fringe. Pierce holes around top for drawstring (thong). Fringe may be dampened and twisted old-style!

© 1992 BY JOEL MONTURE

whip-stitched together. When the bag or pouch is turned right side out, there will be a broad band of hide protruding from the seam, which is then uniformly cut into fringe. The fringe, traditionally, is lightly moistened in the mouth and stretched with the teeth, then each individual fringe thong is rolled across the thigh to create a twisted fringe. This was often rubbed with powdered trade paint or wrapped at the base with a dyed porcupine quill.

A series of uniform holes are pierced along the top of the pouch and a thong run through them (the ends of the thong are cut to a point that is moistened and twisted like a needle). They exit from the same hole in the middle of the back top edge, and draw the pouch closed.

The awl case is a tapering tube of hide fitted to the diameter and length of the awl. It has either a sliding tubular style top, or a flap that falls over the top opening. In either case, it usually has a beaded tab on the narrow bottom end and very often beaded or quilled thongs that hang from it with beauty and motion, often with tin cones (jingles) and dyed red or yellow horsehair. The typical awl case is fully beaded, although the one-piece style with the tab is frequently beaded only over the seam. The seam is whip-stitched from top to bottom, right side out. Then it is burnished smooth with the seam-flattening tool. The sliding top is a band of hide and a circle of hide whip-stitched together. The top

is beaded just like the bottom (Figure 8).

The knife case (which could also be modified to contain scissors) is also whip-stitched from top to bottom, and a slightly undersized matching pattern of thin deer or elk rawhide is inserted inside the leather case after it is beaded. The top of the knife case is then whip-stitched all around the top of the rawhide liner, using the awl to make holes through both the case and the rawhide.

The first step in beading the beadworker's belt set is the preparation of all materials. Lay out the bead pads on the work board and place approximately one teaspoon of each selected bead color on the pad. Make sure the bead sizes are the same. Rather than threading one needle, thread four or six, doubled, waxed, knots clipped. Set all but one aside so that as the thread runs out, it is possible to continue working without interruption by employing the next threaded needle.

The next consideration when beading on a surface (as opposed to edge work) is laying out the pattern or lines to be beaded. The easiest method is to simply draw the pattern or lines on the leather, but care must be taken to bead over the markings so that they do not show. In the case of rows of solid lazy stitch, one line is all that is required because subsequent rows will buttress together. But parallel, spaced rows would require one drawn line per row. Lakota beadworker Faye Spoonhunter presses down a strip of

FIGURE 8 · AWL CASE DETAIL

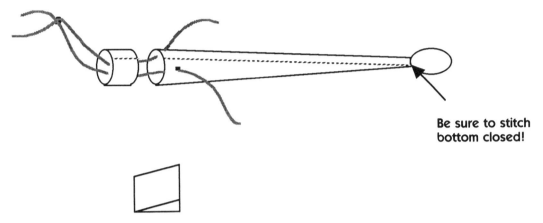

Be sure to stitch bottom closed!

An alternate top is a simple fold of hide stitched up the sides with edge beadwork, with two holes in the top for the thongs.

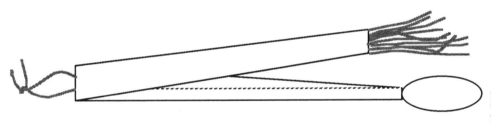

Beaded all around or in a single row up the seam, choose edge beadwork around bottom tab and top flap, and solid beadwork on flap.

© 1992 BY JOEL MONTURE

masking tape and beads perfectly straight parallel lines along the edge of the masking tape without marking the hide. As with pattern making, experience and confidence require less need to mark the hide for beadwork.

∿∿∿∿∿ Lazy Stitch ∿∿∿∿∿

Begin the technique known as *lazy stitch* (so called by anthropologist William C. Orchard in 1929, and later derogatorily retermed "lazy-squaw stitch" by hobbyist/writer Ben Hunt in the 1950s) by using a scrap of hide with a single straight line drawn on it. Hold the hide in your left hand, palm up, with the line running from left to right in front of you. Put the point of the needle in the hide on your side of the line, inserting it just under the surface but not through to the backside of the leather. Bring the point of the needle out exactly on the other side of the line, and pull it all the way through until the knot is snug against the leather. The knot should be a few bead widths from the line.

Place six white beads on your needle and run them down the thread until they are snug against the leather, then lay them flat against the leather in a perpendicular or right angle to the line you marked. The beads will cover the knot. Then put the point of the needle in the hide right below where the thread exits the last bead, and push it through the surface of the leather in a parallel direction to the

line you marked, bringing it out approximately one bead's width from the line of beads you have just tacked down. Repeat with six more white beads, laying them down beside the previous line of beads and sewing them down by running the needle under the hide along the line you marked. In this fashion you will go back and forth building a "row" of beadwork out of lines of beads. See Figures 9 and 10. Figure 9C shows a three-bead row composed of seven lines, and the back-and-forth stitching method. Please note, however, that when stitching, try to bend or "roll" the leather over a finger and push the needle perfectly straight through the hide. Attempting to push the needle down, then bend the needle up and through, will result in bent and broken needles.

The biggest problem for beginners working the lazy-stitch technique is uneven rows and crooked lines. The best way to avoid this is to make sure the lines of beads are "locked" down with tight, even stitches of uniform tension, taking care to space the lines

FIGURE 9 · LAZY-STITCH TECHNIQUES

A

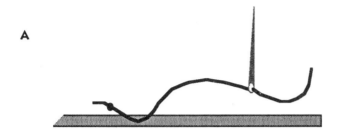

In lazy stitch, the needle and thread pass just under the surface, not through the leather. There are no stitches or knots exposed to wear on the back side of the work.

B

The starting knot is positioned underneath the row.

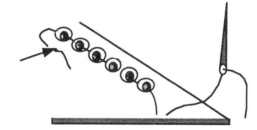

The stitch does not pass through the bottom side of the hide.

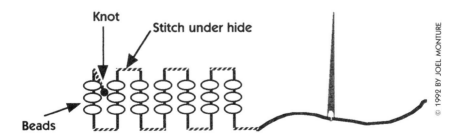

Knot

Stitch under hide

Beads

© 1992 BY JOEL MONTURE

This expanded top view of lazy stitch shows how the starting knot is under the beadwork on the up side, not exposed on the back.

The dotted lines reveal the stitch under the surface of the leather, not through it to be exposed on the back side.

FIGURE 10 · LAZY-STITCH TIPS

A

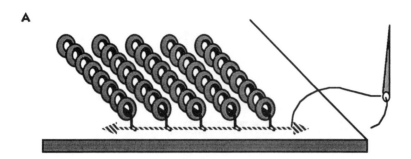

Each line of beads is sewn down, placing the needle along the previous lines of beads as a straight guide.

B

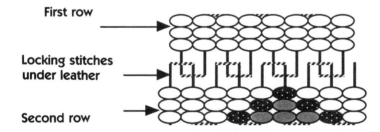

First row

Locking stitches under leather

Second row

In this technique, often used by Cheyenne beadworkers, the stitches of the second row interlock under the leather with the stitches of the first row, drawing the two rows tight together, with no gaps in the finished work. It is done, however, so that the individual lines of beads from row to row align, creating a flatter overall solid beadwork field lacking such obvious rows. It is a stronger beadwork that minimizes the leather stretching out of shape or spaces opening up between the rows.

© 1992 BY JOEL MONTURE

FIGURE 11 · Omaha beadworker Colleen Flores demonstrates how to roll the hide over one's fingers in lazy stitch so that the needle passes straight through the hide. She creates a running line of pink beadwork across the top of the scissors case.

so that they are not bunched up or distorted by previous or subsequent lines within the row. It is also important that you create parallel lines that do not stray at awkward angles, creating gaps where the hide shows between the lines. Of course, there are those times when the row of beadwork is not straight but curved, either in rosette work or in pictographic fill-in. When this occurs, it is necessary to regard the tight curve like the hub of a wheel, and the lines of beads like radiating spokes, which must be spaced farther apart at the wide curve or top and travel from the hub at a right angle. Although lazy stitch is most often thought of as the building block of geometric patterns, it is also used in curvilinear floral patterns, especially among the Great Lakes peoples and the Canadian Cree.

On the rectangular bag the beadwork will be in straight, even rows, but on the rounded bag the beadwork rows will curve, as previously mentioned, around the front perimeter of the hide. There is one distinction between the two bags that is also important in other objects. The rectangular bag is generally beaded after construction and the round bag is beaded before construction, leaving at least ¼ inch of seam allowance for sewing. Some objects are assembled or sewn prior to or after beading. (A complete list is in Appendix 1.)

The first beadwork on the rectangular pouch is a row, from six to ten beads wide, covering the side seams. It should not extend from the start to the finish of the seam but should leave approximately ½ inch of seam exposed on either end. One row is sufficient but three rows create more expansion of pattern and design (see Figure 12).

After the side seams are beaded on the rectangular pouch, a matching band of beadwork is created across the front of the flap that closes the bag. The beadwork should be about a ½ inch from the edge to allow room for holes for the tie thongs.

Next, the front of the bag is beaded in four to six parallel rows of three to five beads, generally in rows of red with double bars of navy/yellow/navy. Or it may be solidly beaded in geometric patterns on white or medium blue backgrounds.

The round fringed pouch may be beaded three ways: The first is a simple row of four to eight beads starting at the top left corner which travel down and around the outside edge of the pouch to the top right corner. Then the interior space may be beaded with parallel rows of four bead lines. The second method is to fill in the interior with solid lazy stitch, and the third method is to create individual patterns of lazy stitch against a hide background. See Figure 13.

Figure 14 demonstrates how a free pattern is created with lazy stitch—"free" referring to the fact that the design elements are not within rows, but beaded directly on the hide. Free patterning or isolated design elements are often added on bordering large area beadwork or used on broad areas of hide, such as dresses or legging flaps, to provide contrast. Small free patterns are also used on the toes or vamps of moccasins as a minor decoration, rather than leaving them completely plain, often in combination with powder trade paint.

The awl case is beaded with a running stitch. Starting at the bottom, insert the needle through the hide of the sewn-up awl case at a right angle to the seam stitching, and begin with six beads. Just like the lazy stitch, the beads are brought over the knot. The object is to wrap beads around and around the case with no breaks in the stitching. Put the needle in the hide exactly where the sixth bead lies, and push the needle back toward your starting stitch, bringing it out between the third and fourth bead. Now, put the needle through the fourth, fifth, and sixth bead, and draw the stitching tight. When you add six more beads and repeat, it will appear as an uninterrupted line of beads wrapping around the case. Refer to Figure 15 to see how the needle goes in a reverse direction and returns back through the beads.

The sliding top, or cover, of the awl case is a continuation of the same pattern, beaded with the same technique. If the cover of the awl case is a flap,

FIGURE 12 · EXAMPLES OF SEAM BEADING ON SQUARE POUCH

One row

One row

Three rows

COLOR CHART

Navy blue

Medium blue

Light blue

Yellow

Pink

Red white-hearts

Light green

Dark green

White

Black

© 1992 BY JOEL MONTURE

FIGURE 13

A

A beaded border and a series of parallel lines beaded horizontally

B

A beaded border and parallel adjacent rows of solid-fill beadwork

C

Design elements created with open lazy stitch

© 1992 BY JOEL MONTURE

FIGURE 14 · LAZY-STITCH DETAILS

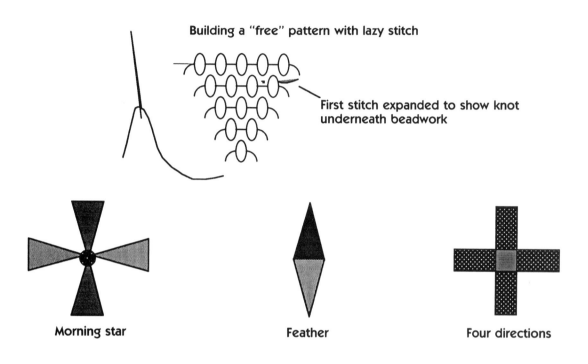

Building a "free" pattern with lazy stitch

First stitch expanded to show knot underneath beadwork

Morning star

Feather

Four directions

FIGURE 15 · RUNNING STITCH

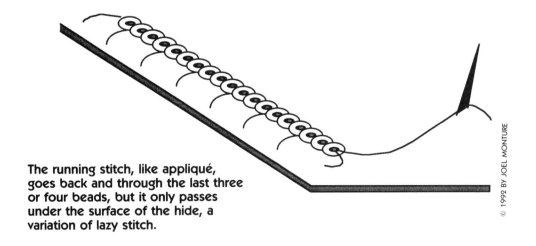

The running stitch, like appliqué, goes back and through the last three or four beads, but it only passes under the surface of the hide, a variation of lazy stitch.

© 1992 BY JOEL MONTURE

FIGURE 16

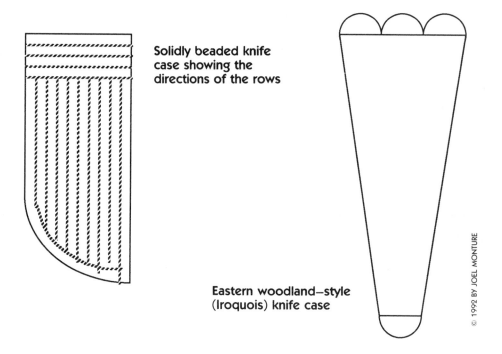

Solidly beaded knife case showing the directions of the rows

Eastern woodland–style (Iroquois) knife case

© 1992 BY JOEL MONTURE

then standard lazy stitch is employed, using the same colors and a repeating pattern or variation of the pattern.

The western-style knife case (or modified as a scissors case) is all lazy stitch in broad rows of solid beadwork. The rows, from three to six depending on the complexity of the pattern, travel horizontally across the top approximately one-third of the way down, and then the rows travel vertically along the borders of the case on either side. Then the rows fill in the interior vertically (Figure 16).

The knife case has a special connotation that was demonstrated by a Lakota beadwork student, Jodi Archambault, who wanted very much to make a belt set to wear with her traditional clothing when she danced. Her grandmother told her she could not wear a knife case unless she knew how to use a knife properly—meaning that she should know how to skin, flesh hides, and butcher the meat. We arranged a time and obtained a beaver from a trapper, and she skinned it, butchered it, fleshed the pelt, and put the knife in the beaded case she made. Her grandmother was pleased and honored because tradition was respected.

This is a valuable and important distinction—the traditional art that Native people create is not only beautiful but functional. Art serves a purpose, which is to enhance our appreciation of life. The wearing of a knife and case is to imply that you know how to use it, just as the wearing of a carpenter's tool belt suggests some skill in woodworking. And, in appreciation of those skills, we create beauty for our tools, whether an awl or knife, or a bag for fleshers and elk antler scrapers. Great amounts of love, time, and patience are expended on our work, because it reflects how we feel about ourselves. It is also the way we provide examples to our children about taking the time to create, to build with our hands, and to be responsible for our endeavors. A successful and prolific beadworker, tradi-tionally, was an industrious person, and a family's wealth was often measured by the amount of beadwork displayed.

As you begin your beadwork, you may wish to consider the advice given by Colleen Flores, a beadworker from the Omaha nation, who was advised always to keep her beadwork covered up when not working on it. The reasoning is that you will be unhappy with your designs because they will always be staring back at you. If you keep your work covered, every time you return to it, it will please you and fill you with joy! It may also be that others shouldn't see or judge your work until it is completed.

EDGE BEADING

Edge beading is an important and necessary finishing or joining technique that is found throughout many nations in North America, from the straps on bandolier bags of the Great Lakes to Tlingit octopus bags of Alaska; Iroquois clothing edges and moccasin flaps; rosette rims on Kiowa and Southern Plains otter fur turbans; the tops of pipe bags and tobacco pouches; and dozens of other applications. Edge beading is the perfect garnish on a piece of beadwork, and is especially valuable combined with ribbon-bound cloth edges. Frequently it may be the only beadwork technique used on a piece in conjunction with paint on hide.

The two most common forms of edge beading are the simple two-bead edging and the rolled edging, which have variations to create different effects.

The two-bead edging creates the effect of European lace, especially when white beads are used. This may actually have been the original intent and influence among the eastern nations, especially the Abenaki and Iroquois, whose first contact with and use of beads was in the seventeenth and eighteenth centuries. An entire thesis might well be developed concerning the development of white-bead-only beadwork in lace patterns on European trade cloth, and the subsequent modes of fashion and applied decoration among eastern nations that gave rise to unique art forms. Often it is thought that the early line quillwork in floral-like patterns was the natural predecessor of floral beadwork, but it was more likely a cross-culturalization of Native artistic expression and European lace fashion during early contact years. (It should also be understood that enormous quantities of lace, ribbons, and cloth twill tapes were stocked as trade goods by merchants or were given as gifts to Native people, as well as woolen strouds and baize, cotton two-color calicoes, linens, and silks.)

The two-bead edging begins, as does all beadwork, with a doubled, waxed, and knotted threaded needle. Insert the needle through the edge of the hide (or ribbon-bound cloth edge) at a right angle and pick up three beads. The needle is then inserted through the hide again, spaced approximately the width of one bead from the knot. The needle then enters the underside of the last bead passing through it again, and drawing the beads tightly against the edge of the hide or cloth. From this point on, the process is repeated, only with *two* beads instead of three, and the effect is that of a flat row of beads lying on the edge topped with a sawtooth-like row of beads standing up (Figure 17). Note that the stitches may be spaced close together so that the top beads ride high and the bottom beads have no spaces between them—or the bottom bead stitches may be farther apart

so that the top beads set down against the edge as well, creating a tighter, less exposed row of beadwork.

A variation on the "sawtooth" pattern of two-bead edging is to use three, four, or more beads to create a different edge appearance. However, it is a looser style of beadwork. The plain two-bead edge technique, though, can be used to also sew two pieces of hide together, such as an unfringed pouch, because the space between the stitches—one bead—is the same as sewing up the pouch without beads, and it is not necessary to double-stitch a seam. Sewing a seam, then edge-beading it, requires double the time and work without added benefit.

It should be noted that there are many contemporary edge techniques that create even more elaborate, lacy results, but these are not traditional. They are more within the realm of Victorian beadwork—such as purses, etc.—that are not Native, though some of them have been adopted for the tourist market.

The rolled edging creates a solid firm border around an edge, either on a pouch, top of a bag, or another open object such as an arrow quiver or knife case. The use of colors creates very little actual patterns, but divides the row into blocks or fields of colors that most often relate to or duplicate the colors in the main body of beadwork on the object. Begin rolled edging with the threaded needle, and insert the needle through the edge of the hide about two bead widths down from the top. The thickness of the hide

FIGURE 17 · EDGE BEADING TECHNIQUES

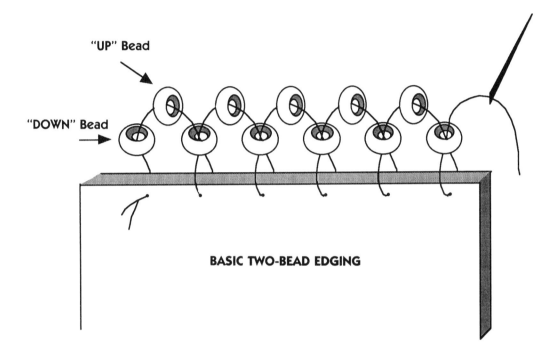

"UP" Bead

"DOWN" Bead

BASIC TWO-BEAD EDGING

HIGH/LOW TECHNIQUES

"UP" bead riding high on
top of down beads

LOOSER STYLE

"UP" bead set between the down beads,
due to wider stitch spacing

TIGHTER STYLE

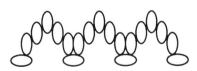

An alternative is to use more than one "UP"
bead to create a looping effect along the edge.

© 1992 BY JOEL MONTURE ALL RIGHTS RESERVED

© 1992 BY LARRY McNEIL

FIGURE 17A · Maudie King is doing two-bead edging on a black-dyed, brain-tanned deer-hide strap for a traditional shoulder bag. Note how the stitches are far apart, allowing the "up" bead to sit down against the hide (see text for detailed explanation). The needle passes just beneath the edge of the hide so the length of the stitches is short and tight without distorting the leather.

© 1992 BY LARRY McNEIL

FIGURE 17B · Colleen Flores, an Omaha beadworker, demonstrates locking down the final beads in a line across the top of the scissors case. The scissors case was stitched together using the two-bead edging technique.

© 1992 BY LARRY McNEIL

FIGURE 17C · Once the "sky dome" border is created, Maudie goes back creating two small lines like sprouts. Here, one has been done and she is setting the needle, already threaded with three beads, to create the second line. Note carefully that the side seam of the bag is sewn up (closed) with two-bead edging only, which continues around the top flap of the bag. A good, tight two-bead edge technique is as strong a sewing method as sewing the bag first, then beading the edge later, but you skip a step and save time.

and the actual size of the beads will determine how many beads you will use, and this requires a little practice, experience, and judgment by the beadworker. Try hard. We will assume that six beads are required, which are brought down the thread to the back side of the hide, and then rolled over the top edge to the front side of the hide that is facing you (Figure 18). The needle is then put through the hide again, one bead width to the right of the first stitch. Another six beads are added and the stitch repeated. In this manner, the beads are rolled from back to front, creating a solid rolled edge of beadwork, with a general pattern of bars of solid color broken up by individual lines of contrasting color in repetitive designs. Unlike the two-edge technique, rolled edging tends to stretch the hide and open up the tops of pouches, which is normal and not of concern. Even more attractive, when the bag top is closed with a thong and the rolled edge is uniformly gathered, the effect is like that of a flower blossom in full bead bloom.

A variation of the rolled edge is to space the stitches so that the lines of beadwork are separated at angles that create a "barber pole" effect of open hide and stripes of sparkling glass beads!

FIGURE 18 · ROLLED EDGE BEADWORK

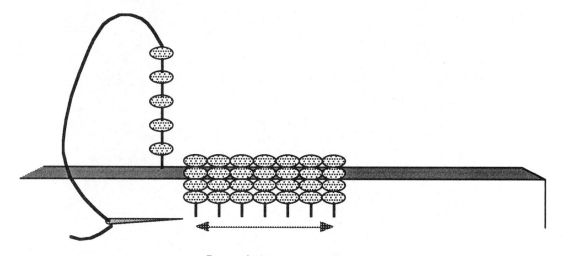

Even stitches along edge

Side view showing how beads
are wrapped around the edge
of the hide

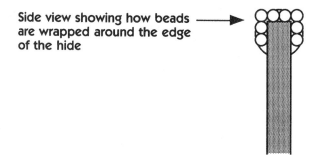

Line edging at an angle with wide spacing

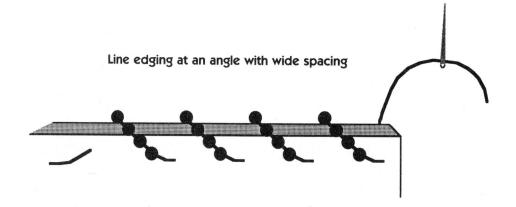

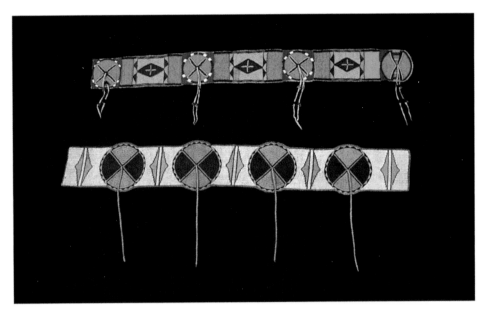

Plate 1: Blanket bands: (*top*) A Crow blanket band circa 1890. *Bottom:* A Lakota (Sioux) blanket band circa 1870. A blanket, or buffalo robe, was as much a garment for everyday wear and use as moccasins, and was commonly ornamented with a row or band of beadwork, generally with spaced rosettes. Worn horizontally around the waist, like a belt. The origin of the style came from the practice of splitting unwieldy buffalo hides down the spine to be tanned in two pieces, which were later sewn up and the seam covered with a row or strip of quillwork. The style evolved to include rosettes, and eventually more rows, until the art form became a significant one of very wide colorful bands.

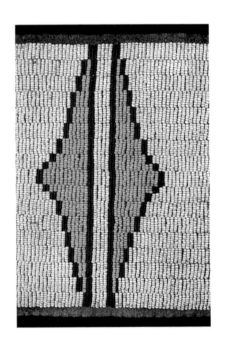

All photographs © Larry McNeil, 1992

All articles pictured appear courtesy of Morning Star Gallery, Ltd.,
Santa Fe, New Mexico, unless otherwise noted.

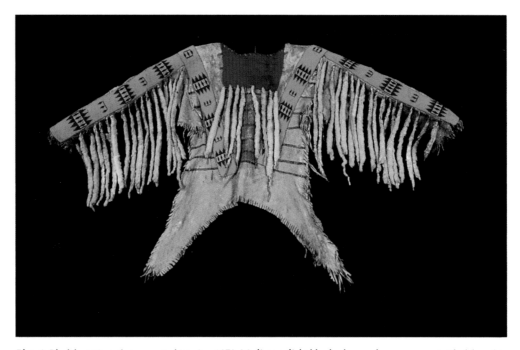

Plate 2: Blackfoot/Assiniboine man's shirt, circa 1870. Medium or light blue backgrounds are common in Blackfoot shirt and legging strips. Pictured is a standard style, with ermine "tail" drops and wool yoke/bib. The blue and yellow trade paint are further emphasized by brown horizontal lines, which create an even greater sense of movement in the garment.

Plate 3: Lakota (Sioux) shirt, circa 1860. An example of quillwork, the predecessor of beadwork. Quillwork is sewn on separate strips that are then sewn to a shirt. The shirt is rubbed with blue and yellow trade paint, quill-wrapped hair locks are added down the front and back of the shoulder strips, and to the backside of the arm strips. (This is actually the back of the shirt—both front and back are identical.) A yoke or bib is added and the neck opening bound with trade cloth or a two-color calico.

Plate 4: Crow man's shirt, circa 1890. Traditional Crow bead colors in a variation of hourglass design make this a standard-style shirt with twisted ermine fur "tails" wrapped with red wool and a red wool beaded yoke/bib. No white lines—the patterns are all blocks of solid color.

Plate 5: Cheyenne girl's dress, circa 1885. A very nice example of a classic Cheyenne-style dress, but with a unique difference—it has beaded belt loops (very rare) in imitation of white man's trousers. Additional fringe is added with thongs on the body of the garment, strung with large cobalt blue trade beads. Note the free-design work on the curved bottom row.

Plate 6: Lakota (Sioux) man's shirt, circa 1880. A very rich and beautiful painted "hairlock" shirt with exquisite repeating American flag-over-tipi motifs. Hair locks are wrapped with porcupine quills (colored orange with aniline trade dye), and the neckline is bound with printed cotton calico. A classical shirt style.

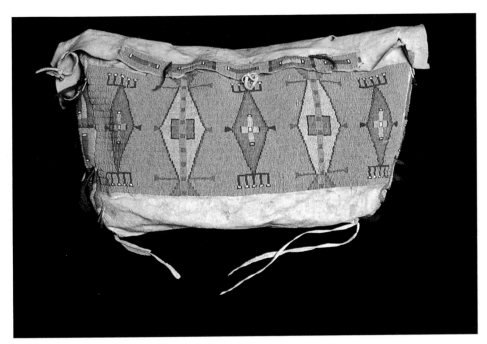

Plate 7: Lakota (Sioux) possible bag, circa 1880–90. A typical design square-bottom bag with vertical side-seam beading and horizonal panel beading on the front that extends right to the sides. Notice that the top-flap beading matches the side seams, and unifies the design with the same colors as the front beading. The very small use of white (like the use of cut metal beads in similar fashion) brightens the entire appearance of the bag. These are classic colors used in an unconventional way—the broad yellow fields for example, and the reverse red/blue outlines of the major design elements. A truly wonderful and striking creation!

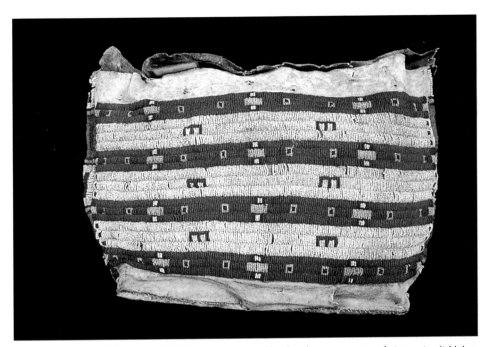

Plate 8: Lakota possible bag, circa 1890. Twenty-one rows of beadwork create an extremely interesting field that initially seems busy, but is only composed of bars and square, no diagonals! The six red "Tridents" focus attention to the center of the work—without them the viewer would be drawn back and forth along the horizontal rows. Very well designed.

Plate 9: Reverse of number ten, except the pattern is asymmetrical, both in color and design. The four pink and transparent navy leaves across the bottom unify the whole design.

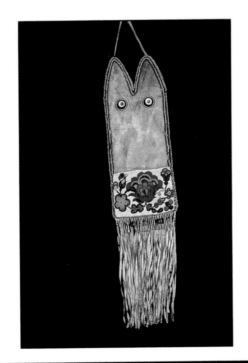

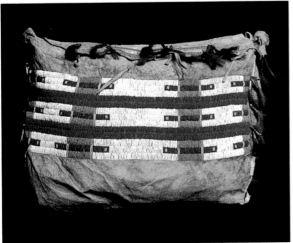

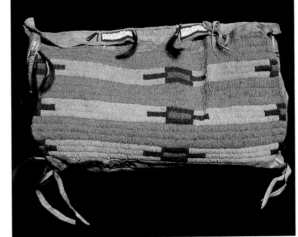

Plate 10: Cree pipe bag, circa 1890. Beaded on hide, the top of the bag is dark navy wool edged with yellow cotton. The beadwork is a symmetrical pattern suggestive of early Pennsylvania Dutch fracktur paintings that found their way west. The colors in floral beadwork were often more varied than those in western or southern plains geometrics, perhaps because floral patterns are not so standardized, and unusual colors in small amounts were employed only once or twice. This bag is created with the running backstitch or overlaid spot stitch.

Plate 12: Lakota (Sioux) possible bag, circa 1880. An interesting design made up of two greens, yellow, and blue on a white field. The flap and sides contain the red and pale blue, offset with tin cones (jingles) and red-dyed horsehair. The great appeal of this design, found also in possible-bag designs of other nations, is the horizontal effect broken up by the vertical bar motifs in contrasting colors. Even at a distance no color is lost on the viewer.

Plate 11: Cree pipe bag, circa 1870. The quillwork suggests this bag may be Blackfoot, but the edge beadwork up the sides is atypical. An interesting feature is the cast metal buttons (four-hole Civil War military style) with rosette-style beadwork around them at the top. The floral pattern is suggestive of early hooked rugs, which were in fashion at the time.

Plate 13: Lakota (Sioux) possible bag, circa 1880. Side panels are a variant match of top-flap beading. This is a bold pattern with unusual amounts of yellow, and interesting for its arrangement because the bottom is solid yellow. The eighteen rows are fairly wide, with ten bead lines. An eight-bead line rearrangement would have narrowed the pattern enough to include three more lines of blue across the bottom for symmetry, however the appeal lies in its asymmetrical dimensions.

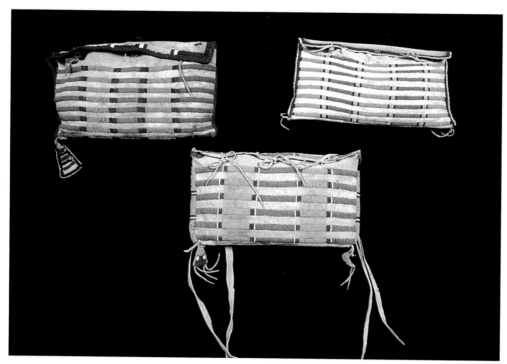

Plate 14: Three small Crow possible bags, circa 1880. The uniqueness of these three similar bags is that each has a different side-seam treatment: the top right has plain red trade wool bound over the seam and around the top flap; the top left has red wool bindings with two-bead edging; the bottom bag has a rolled-bead edging similar to the top of a pipe bag. Also, they do not have a square-bottom seam, but are sewn flat, like an envelope. Although not probable, they could almost all have been made by the same person. These three bags illustrate well that the same design is virtually limitless given the wide color options available. The bottom bag also shows how dramatic a single line of white beads is against a dark row.

Plate 15: Four eastern needle cases: (*top left*) Seneca, circa 1880; (*top right*) Mohawk, circa 1900; (*lower left*) Great Lakes, circa 1890. The red wool has been completely devoured by moths, revealing a stiff paper backing; (*lower right*) Passamaquoddy, circa 1870. Dyed moose hair embroidery on black deerskin (author's collection).

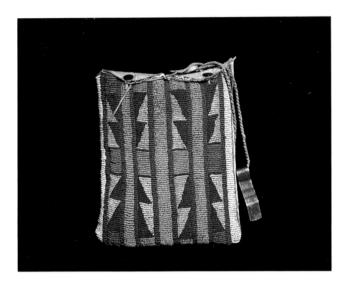

Plate 16: A Crow mirror bag, with twisted thong and metal pincers (tweezers) for removing facial hair, circa 1880. A variation on the double-hourglass design, and suggestive of parfleche (painted rawhide) elements. Note how the bead count varies in the individual vertical rows and how the contrast of simple design elements creates a complex pattern. Also note the two brass button closures.

Plate 17: Lakota (Sioux), circa 1890–1900. Like shirt or legging strips, this bag has separate hide beadwork panels applied to a stiff rawhide base made from domestic calf with traces of hair remaining on the hide. The almost lime-colored transparent beads indicate a wider variety of later bead trade—such colors were more common in eastern Great Lakes works. The contrast between the white and green fields and the two separately attached blue-based tabs beneath the ties creates a striking expression. Rawhide "pockets" like these were often painted and called parfleche and frequently hung from tipi poles or walls.

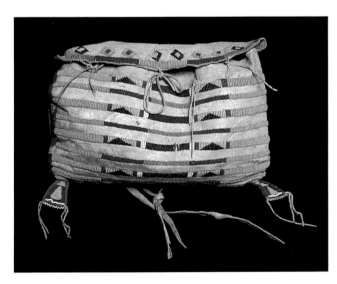

Plate 18: Medium-sized Crow possible bag, circa 1890–1900. A very classic Crow style with contrasting hide between the parallel horizontal rows, although the effect is akin to full-panel beading. This example is made more elaborate by the triangle motifs within the bands, which produce more movement. The top flap is also elaborated with free-pattern designs along the flap strip, which alternates the colors of the main front beading.

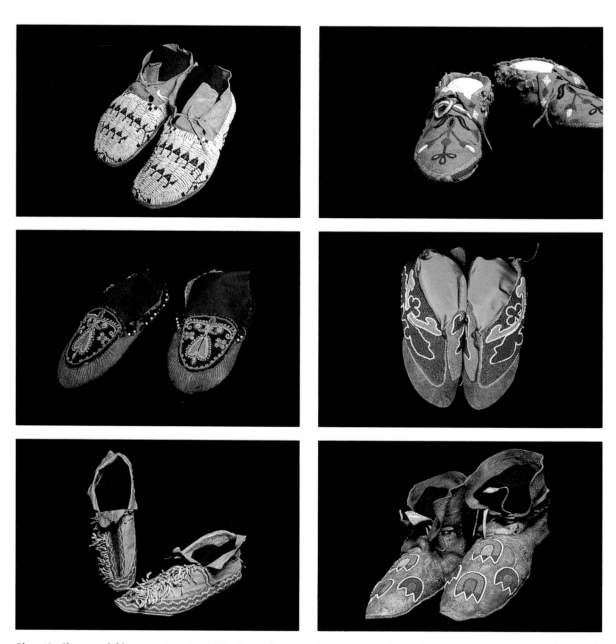

Plate 19: Cheyenne child's moccasins, circa 1880. Extraordinarily crisp, clean beadwork of only three colors (unusual) and in a strikingly stark but effective pattern.

Plate 21: Micmac moccasins from New Brunswick or eastern Maine, circa 1890–1910. Uniformly puckered soft-sole moccasins with U-shaped vamps (uppers) beaded with different size beads, red wool welt trim around vamps, and blue wool narrow flaps and vamp backing. Typical late eastern colors also popular in Victorian beadwork of the period. Note the heart motif used extensively in floral work.

Plate 23: Arapahoe moccasins, circa 1880. Side fringing, yellow and blue trade paint rubbed into the hide, and dramatic two-color matching beadwork with lightning pattern makes this pair very striking. Kiowa, Comanche, and Jicarilla Apache make similar styles, often with thick clusters of tin cone jingles on the fringe ends.

Plate 20: Fort Peck Assiniboine moccasins, circa 1880. Striking for the use of transparent and semi-transparent beads, unusual colors, and bold contrasts. Note how the tongue is geometric over the floral uppers.

Plate 22: Soft-soled moccasins attributed as "Prairie," circa 1870. Very indicative of the opposite-flap style common among Pottawatomie, Sac, and Fox. Notice how the flaps match in reverse.

Plate 24: Crow floral beaded moccasins, circa 1880. A very nice example of curvilinear and angular components in floral work with dramatic white outlines, and good contrasting fill-in color. An outstanding feature of these moccasins is the two-layer blue and red saw-tooth cut trade wool, inserted into the seam of the added on high tops—a wonderful personal touch.

Plate 25: Two pairs of Arapahoe moccasins, circa 1870. Dramatically demonstrates how hide color brings out the contrast in beads. Note how the red and yellow bottom trim border extends around the outside, but not completely around the inside of the moccasins—the area which rubs up against the underside of a horse.

Plate 26: Two pairs of moccasins. Apache, circa 1880. Subtlely beaded sole borders and pale green trade paint in the open area along the centers: (right) Cree, circa 1870. Very unusual example of beadwork with all white and only two shades of blue. Note the fine crosses within the bottom sole row and the striped calico cloth tops.

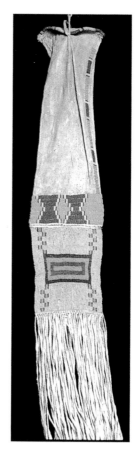

Plate 27: Lakota (Sioux) pipe bag, circa 1870. A very rare and unusual style with a loomed or woven technique beaded panel below the bag instead of quill-wrapped rawhide fringe.

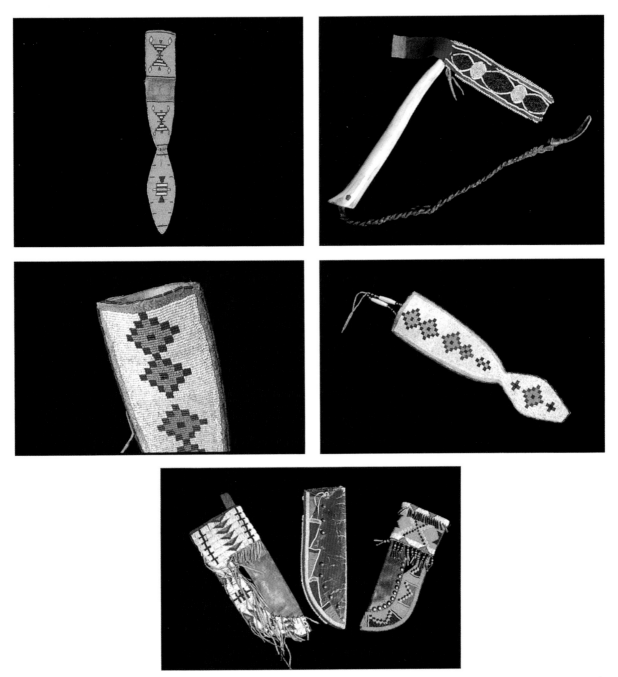

Plate 28: Blackfoot Beavertail dagger case, circa 1870. An exceptionally beautiful knife/dagger case containing cut brass beads as secondary design fill and crisp white two-bead edging on a dramatic field of plain hide.

Plate 30: Detail showing the rawhide liner and the edge-beading technique.

Plate 32: Three knife cases, circa 1880: (*from left to right*) Blackfoot on commercial or boot-top leather with hide fringe; Crow painted rawhide with fold-over top flap and brass beads (note the white edge beading); Blackfoot on commercial or boot-top leather, with brass tacks, hollow brass beads, and tin cone jingles.

Plate 29: Osage quirt (horse crop or whip), circa 1890. Used extensively by horse-culture nations, horse quirts were typically made of a long elk antler tine, with a braided whip (often two), and a beaded wrist strap. This strap is layered red trade cloth with the white selvage edge over hide, ornamented with two-bead edging in white and a semi-geometric pattern reminiscent of ribbon work, also popular among the Osage. It is common to find similar patterning in different media, for instance rawhide painted designs and beadwork.

Plate 31: Cree dagger case, circa 1890. An impressive white field makes the star pattern burst out, and a tight-edge technique of alternating reds (white-lined) and navy create an eye-catching design.

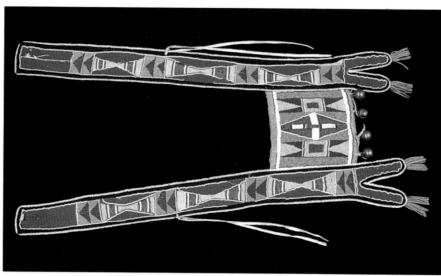

Plate 35: Crow horse gear, circa 1890. Sometimes referred to as a martingale, this is a crupper that hangs from around the horse's neck like a bib against its chest. Beaded on blue and red trade cloth, the use of white beads is a good example of contrast, dividing all the main color areas. The sparse use of yellow in only the "bib" area makes it all that much more outstanding. Green-painted thong forms the tassles on the tabs. Note the sleigh bells.

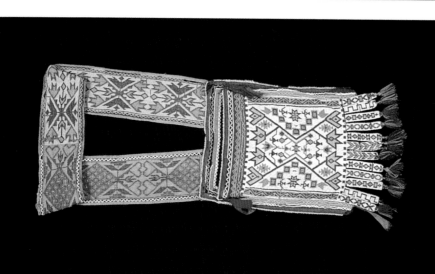

Plate 34: Great Lakes bandolier bag, circa 1880. Although this shoulder bag is of the same style as Plate 28, there are significant differences. The appliqué line work is achieved with colored beads on green twill tape bindings, and the bottom fringe appearance is created with narrow loom-beaded bands of six distinctly different pairs of designs. Note the bird effigies in the main body design, arranged in the four directions or quarters, and the use of "heart" shapes.

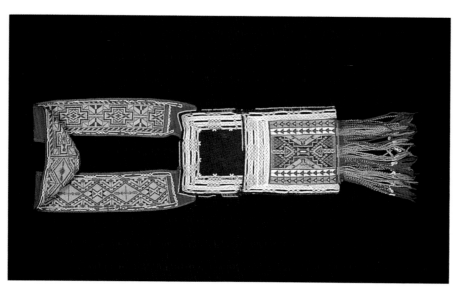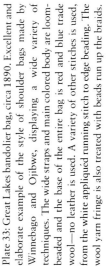

Plate 33: Great Lakes bandolier bag, circa 1890. Excellent and elaborate example of the style of shoulder bags made by Winnebago and Ojibwe, displaying a wide variety of techniques. The wide straps and main colored body are loom-beaded and the base of the entire bag is red and blue trade wool—no leather is used. A variety of other stitches is used, from the white appliquéd running stitch to edge beading. The wool yarn fringe is also treated with beads run up the braids.

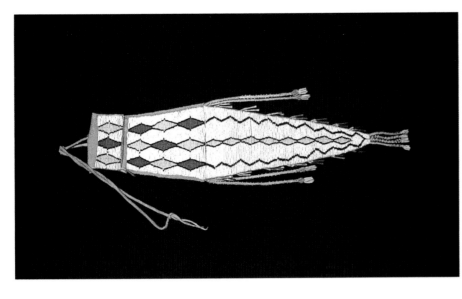

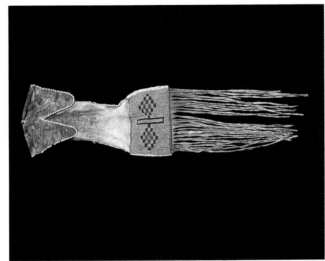

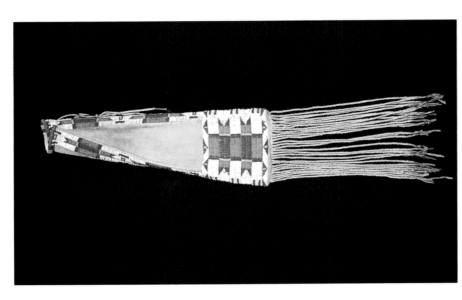

Plate 38: Ute "tail" pouch, circa 1880. The diamond pattern overflap closure, which matches the body of the pouch, and a tapering tail with beaded thongs and tin cones (jingles) are the highlights of this work. A plain running or overlaid spot stitch with a watery effect as the main pattern extends into the "tail."

Plate 37: Blackfoot pipe bag, circa 1870. A wonderful example of a tab-top bag with two-bead edging. The white rolled edging on the body of the bag and the vertical running stitch create the main design. Notice that the bottom section of the bag is of a darker, thicker leather, perhaps buffalo, and the top has been added, made of a thinner lighter leather, perhaps deer or elk. The top was originally the same width but has stretched over time from the weight of the pipe or other contents. Also note that the sides of the top of the bag are stitched with sinew with two beads placed on every loop of the whip stitch. An interesting possibility is that the significantly darker lower hide may in fact be part of a smoke-darkened buffalo hide tipi cover, which was often cut up for beadwork or garments. In any event, it was common for pipe bags to be made from two pieces of hide, top and bottom, with the beadwork coming right up to the edge of the seam.

Plate 36: Arapahoe pipe bag, circa 1860. Although this bag has an Arapahoe attribution, its style and colors are commonly found among the Cheyenne, and has been called the "caterpillar" pattern. Arapahoe and Cheyenne people had a close relationship, and many designs overlapped. It's possible that this piece was obtained from an Arapahoe community, but made by a Cheyenne member or relative.

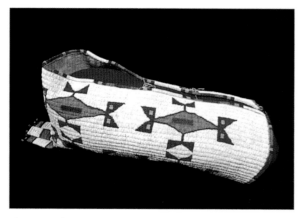

Plate 39: Lakota (Sioux) cradleboard cover, circa 1880. One of the most respected beadwork forms, and a crowning achievement, was a beautiful cradleboard or baby carrier cover, which honored a new member of the family and community. This example is a classic in all details—broad field of white so typical in Lakota work, contrasts of dark colors, forked triangles and diamonds, and rolled-edge beadwork with bands of color. A magnificent display of the art of beadwork!

Plate 40: Strike-A-Light pouches, circa 1870–80: *(from left to right)* Lakota, 1890; Apache, 1880; Lakota, 1870. Strike-A-Light pouches were used to carry flint and steel for lighting fires, wooden matches, or often ration coupons. All three examples shown are made from commercial leather, possibly boot tops, and are beaded on the smooth or hair side. Fringe is added, with tin cone jingles.

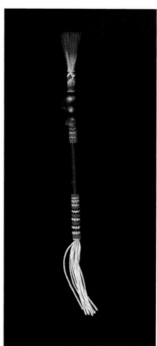

Plate 43: Iroquois woman's wraparound skirt and leggings created by Cindy Monture in 1989.

Plate 41: Traditional woman's awl case created by Cindy Monture, 1992.

Plate 42: Peyote stitchwork on a gourd rattle (author's collection).

Running Stitch and
== Variation Spot Stitch ==

Among many nations, the running or two-thread spot stitch is used to create broad areas of solid beadwork. Examples include the Crow and Blackfoot geometric patterns, and Great Lakes and Alaskan floral work. The reason for this method is because lazy stitch results in rows of from eight to twelve beads, while the running or spot stitch results in long parallel lines of solid beadwork with no rows or ridges. It gives a flatter, more solid appearance, and is a very tight technique. A part of its appeal is that solid areas in geometric patterns can be split (as in Crow work) with a single line of con-trasting beads, usually white running in diagonal directions. The intense hues of glass beads allows even a single line of beads standing in marked opposition to the main-fill color to jump out at the viewer, even at considerable distances. (See color plate of the Crow martingale.) The same is true in floral patterns, from Sac and Fox moccasin flaps to Mohawk Niagara work done on velvet at the turn of the century.

The running stitch is the same technique used to bead the round awl case, but in this instance it is used on flat surfaces to create curvilinear designs or long straight lines (Figure 19). This is also called "appliqué" work when done with two threads (Figure 19). The running stitch beadwork is created by sewing down from four to eight beads, with the stitch passing through the hide or cloth in a reverse direction along the line of beads, coming back out through the middle of the bead count, then the needle passing back through the last beads. If there are six beads, the needle will pass through the last three; if there are eight, it will go through four, etc. In this technique on a flat surface, very fine curves and angles can be fashioned, including enclosed abstract or realistic floral patterns or the outlines of pictographic representations, much like the Cheyenne River Lakota courting scenes on pipe bags or saddlebags. It is common to combine techniques—the curvilinear floral or pictographic designs may be enclosed by a field of solid lazy stitch in rows, or it may be enclosed by solid lines of running stitch.

Once a curvilinear design is outlined with running stitches, the interior is filled in with matching or contrasting beads using either lazy stitch or running stitch, depending on the length of the line of beads. If the bead lines exceed twelve beads, it is best to use running stitch; lazy stitch is fine if the bead count is under twelve. (See Figure 20 on building floral patterns.) The reason is that lines or stitches containing more than twelve beads produce a looser, less stable beadwork that is prone to dam-

age with use. Beads that are stitched down tightly in smaller numbers will remain secure.

The two-thread spot stitch is a different way of obtaining the same results. This technique is begun with two threaded needles: One is stitched at the beginning point and strung with as many beads as are necessary to complete the curvilinear design or outline. The second thread is stitched at a point close to the start and serves to whip-stitch down the line of beads, which are kept in tension. The needle enters the hide or cloth at a right angle to the line of beads so that the stitch is barely a thread's width, and falls between the beads. However, it travels along the line of beads at an angle and comes up right under the line four or so beads from the previous stitch. Using the spot stitch gives beadworkers much freedom by allowing them to string perhaps twelve inches or more of beads, and then move the line around the surface to create patterns at will before sewing it down. This is a more abstract method of developing patterns, which relies heavily on instinct and individual choice rather than a preplanned, marked-out design that must be followed, leaving no option for change along the way. The development of patterns and color choice is accomplished in two ways— either before the beadwork begins, with a "mapping" of the route, or in a rather free-form manner, the latter of which is made possible by two-thread spot stitching.

There are different approaches to

FIGURE 19 · TWO-THREAD SPOT STITCH APPLIQUÉ

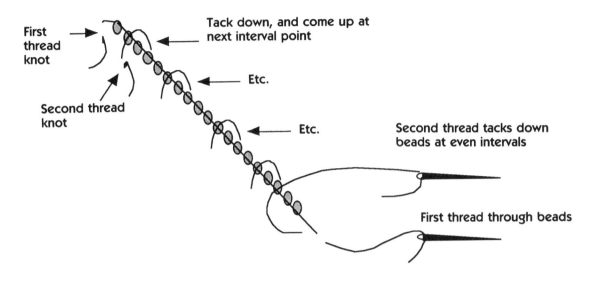

First thread knot

Tack down, and come up at next interval point

Second thread knot

Etc.

Etc.

Second thread tacks down beads at even intervals

First thread through beads

FIGURE 20 · APPLIQUÉ BASICS

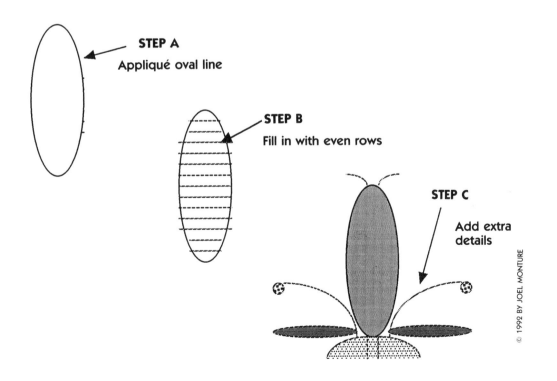

STEP A
Appliqué oval line

STEP B
Fill in with even rows

STEP C
Add extra details

© 1992 BY JOEL MONTURE

several of these techniques. All them can be done lazy-stitch style with the thread passing just under the surface of the hide, although some people pass the needle and thread completely through, creating many stitches on the back side. These exposed stitches need to be protected with a lining of muslin, linen, or calico on the inside of a mirror bag, for example. (Mirror bags, especially Crow, were beaded front and back, often with a cutout area on the front like a picture frame, which revealed the mirror.)

It is also common on some northern Cree (and other) beadwork to back the hide with paper or waxed paperboard (such as found in butter boxes) to prevent the hide from stretching out of shape. The beadworker chooses tight floral patterns where the stitches go in all directions. The exposed stitches on the bottom of the paper are covered with a layer of hide—for instance, on the U-shaped upper vamp of moccasins—that prevents wear on the stitches.

These are the basic techniques—lazy stitch; running or spot (overlaid) appliqué; edge sawtooth or rolled—that are used in 90 percent of most Native American beaded art. Anthropologists William Wildschut and John Ewers describe the combination of lazy stitch, which passes just under the hide, with the running backstitch, which goes back and then through the beads again to produce long lines or curved designs: the *modified lazy stitch*. But they regionalize that term by further narrowing it to *Crow stitch*. This is inappropriate because many other nations did and do use this technique—the Blackfoot, Nez Percé, Plains Cree, etc.—and the term *running backstitch* adequately describes the technique without, shall we say, leaving anyone out. However, the use of this technique by the Crow is of the highest level, both in superior designs and patterns and in the significantly large pieces, especially in beaded horse trappings and gear, saddles, and cruppers.

PEYOTE STITCH

Developed among the southern Plains nations during the late nineteenth and early twentieth centuries, the *peyote stitch* is so called because of its association with and predominance in ceremonial objects used by the Native American Church, which employs the sacred peyote cactus. Such objects as wing bone whistles, rattles, and fans with loose groupings of feathers are beaded with this technique, although contemporary items like earrings are also beaded in this manner. Usually very small beads, from size 13/0 to 18/0 are used, and often cut (faceted) beads are added for even more beauty. This technique, more than any other,

requires an absolute uniformity of bead size to produce even-quality work, and not just within the same group. All the bead color sizes need to be matched exactly, because the finished work will be uneven otherwise.

Begin with a round object—a stick or rattle handle—and glue or stitch a covering of soft leather around the area to be beaded. Make sure the vertical seam of the leather is burnished flat to avoid any ridges bulging up the beadwork. Now with a doubled and waxed thread, make a stitch at the top of the bead area bringing the thread out at the top (Figure 21). Pick up as many beads as will wrap tightly

FIGURE 21 · PEYOTE/GOURD STITCH

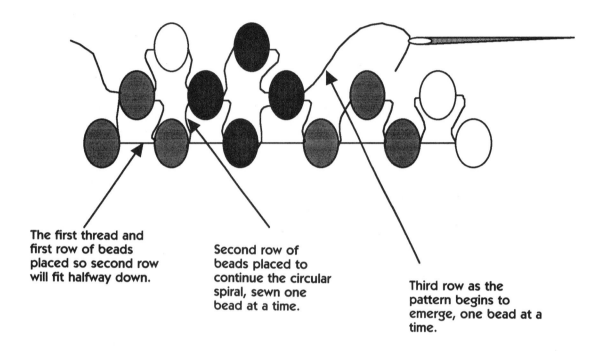

The first thread and first row of beads placed so second row will fit halfway down.

Second row of beads placed to continue the circular spiral, sewn one bead at a time.

Third row as the pattern begins to emerge, one bead at a time.

All peyote stitch patterns are created on the diagonal, and require bold contrasts to stand out distinctly.

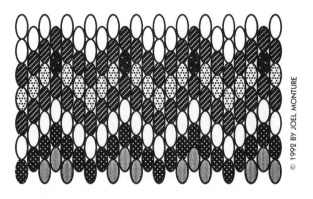

© 1992 BY JOEL MONTURE

around the cylindrical object. Holding them with tension, count them, then release and remove exactly half the beads. If there is an odd number in the total count—for instance, twenty-five, remove thirteen for a remaining count of twelve. The number of beads that go around the object may be either an even number like twelve or an odd number like fifteen, but the even/odd choice may influence the type of patterns you can create. For beginners, it is best to work out patterns on special graph paper, because this technique is very time-consuming and it is frustrating to realize that a pattern out of your head is not lining up right after the initial start-up.

Wrap the beads now around the object, spacing them one bead width apart until they completely circle the object. Bring the needle through the first bead to complete the circle. Pick up one new bead and bring the needle through the second bead, setting the new bead down between the first and second bead. Continue with another new bead, bringing the needle

through the third bead. In this fashion—adding one bead at a time to create a second row—the first row will be interlocked. There are no stitches through leather, but rather a weaving of beads on thread with leather as the buffer between the wood, bone, antler, or feather base. This style is reminiscent of the Victorian beaded clutch purses at the turn of the century. Peyote stitch work requires much patience, but the diagonal or linear pattern possibilities are endless, from feather motifs to lightning zigzags.

John Whitecloud, a noted peyote stitcher and dancer, once commented that an uncle told him that five colors was the most appropriate number, as they related to the five states of a well-ordered mind. John showed me a piece of work he had done with fourteen colors, saying, "I had a lot on my mind that day!" But it is true that beadwork is a reflection of your feelings, and it is best, for beadwork to be good, to think only good thoughts and speak well of others while doing your work.

LOOMWORK

The rise of imported Native American–style loom beadwork and its low cost have devalued much of the real art and relegated it to a back corner. However, the early Native loomwork cannot be matched by machines, nor does most modern loomwork approach the intricacies of pattern and colors. Perhaps some of the finest loomwork occurs on the elaborate bandolier-style shoulder bags of the Great Lakes nations, also in combination with trade wool cloth and yarnwork. The richness of these bags is found in the ornate designs and multiple geometrics that are also present in oriental rugs.

Similar to peyote stitch, loomwork is woven with only a needle and thread, and without the benefit of a base of leather or cloth. When the beadwork is completed, it is sewn down on the object or garment, with the loose warp threads tightly knotted and sewn under the ends of the beadwork.

Basically, the loom is constructed to support a series of horizontal "warp" threads that have the beads woven between them with a double "woof" or "weft" thread. Looms have been constructed in many ways, including using an open shoe box with notched ends to support and separate the warp

FIGURE 22 · A SIMPLE BEADWORK LOOM

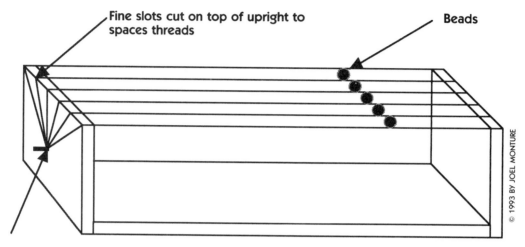

Fine slots cut on top of upright to spaces threads

Beads

© 1993 BY JOEL MONTURE

Nail or peg to tie off threads, or threads can be wrapped around the bottom of the loom in a continuous circle until the desired number of strands is achieved.

threads. An early technique was to use a long stick, curved like a bow, with a perforated strip of rawhide at either end serving as heddles through which the warp threads passed. These heddles were secured tightly to both ends of the bow to maintain tension on the warp. Another loom is constructed simply of a wooden board with a short upright board at either end, the tops of which have an even series of saw cuts—approximately one bead width apart through which the warp threads are passed (Figure 22).

Remember that the loom must be both long enough and wide enough for the completed work.

The loom is warped with a larger thread than the beadwork thread— usually a linen thread—but a button-hole twist thread will do fine. The outside thread is double, but single strands fill in the interior (Figure 23).

Start beading with a long double, waxed needle and thread, tying the bottom end of the thread to the far outside double-warp thread. Pick up enough beads to place one between each warp thread. If the beads are laid on top of the warp (some people prefer to work pressing the beads up from the underside), the needle passes back through each bead on the *underside* of the warp. With a thread passing above and below the warp, each bead is tightly locked between a warp thread. Bring the thread up and over the far side again and repeat the process, gradually building your patterns with the introduction of new colors.

FIGURE 23 · LOOM BEADWORK

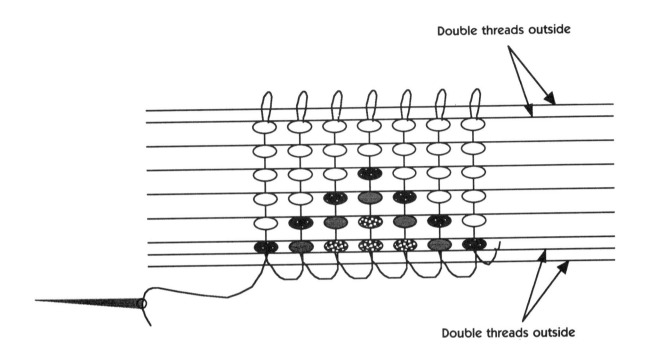

Double threads outside

Double threads outside

DETAIL OF SINGLE LINE OF LOOMWORK

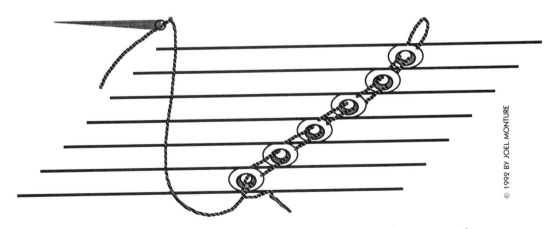

© 1992 BY JOEL MONTURE

The strung beads are first laid on top of the warp threads, with one bead between each warp thread. The needle goes over and under the outside warp and goes back through the beads under the warp threads, forming a weft above and below each warp thread. The process simply repeats itself, and the mathematical arrangements of beads by colors produce a pattern.

Care should be used to keep the lines straight and perfectly aligned with the same tension. When the beadwork is completed, the warp threads are cut, but enough length remains to tie them together: the first thread to the second, the third to the fourth, and so on until the ends are bound. Some people use masking tape on the end threads and fold the tape under the work.

The work is sewn down with a whip stitch that passes through the double outside warp threads on both sides of the work, and with a running stitch on the ends that tacks down each warp thread (taking care to make sure the loose ends of the warp threads are folded under the work).

Looms are widely available from commercial sources, or easily constructed with a little imagination to suit individual needs.

ROSETTES

A *rosette*, or solid circle of beadwork, does not necessarily refer to a floral pattern, although later rosettes, especially among the Crow, Plateau, and northern nations, were indeed elaborate floral patterns coordinated to match horse gear.

The true rosette evolved from quilled circles or medallions that were used on garments (shirt fronts); on the outside of lodges (tipis) at the four quarters; on the brow band ends on bonnets or headdresses; on the top of cradle board covers; and on the uppers of moccasins, quivers, and pouches. With a small, open center, a row or band of quillwork was sewn in a circle, then another and another until the desired diameter was achieved. The edge was trimmed away leaving approximately ⅛ inch to sew the rosette down with a whip stitch. Quillwork was sewn in geometric patterns, such as double whirlwinds and four directions, and the early beaded rosettes copied these patterns. This was especially the case in the larger pony beads, the use of which is so well documented in the 1830s paintings of Karl Bodmer.

When seed-beading a rosette in concentric rows, it is important to remember that each line of beads that makes up the row must be aligned, especially in the first and second rows, with tight centers and a slight fanning-out at the edge, the same way the spokes of a wheel fan out at 90 degrees from the hub. This is necessary in all lazy-stitch beadwork in rows that curve: The inside of the curve is tight together and the outside slightly spread open to create the curve.

The second method that evolved was to use concentric rings or lines of running backstitch, starting from a single bead in the center. One bead is stitched down, and the thread brought up on the outside of the bead. Then four beads are backstitched down and the thread brought up between the second and third bead, then through the third and fourth bead. Four more beads will complete the first ring of beads around the center bead; the needle enters the first bead of the ring, then the leather, and comes up just outside the first ring. The second ring of beads is sewn down the same way; however, from six to eight beads may be used, the goal being that the work is secured down every three to four beads. Like the rings in a tree, the rosette grows, and the patterns can be quite intricate. In true appliqué work, the needle passes through the hide and leaves a web of stitches on the back side, which is acceptable if the rosette is to be backed with a second circle of leather or else sewn onto a garment, object, or pouch.

A third, and trickier, technique is to begin with one center bead and create a running backstitch spiral line of

beadwork that continues to grow. Lining up single bead colors in the creation of an intricate pattern is the tricky part, and it requires careful planning.

One pitfall to avoid, even though tight beadwork is desirable, is beading rosettes so tightly as to compress the leather, which will have a cupping effect. The rosette will not lie flat. Often there is a slight rise in the center, which can always be tacked down with an invisible stitch to the backing layer, but overly tight stitching will pull the leather out of shape.

A simple way to find the exact center of a rosette is to fold the circle in half, then in half again as a quarter circle. The point of the wedge can be spotted with a pencil or awl for reference to begin beading.

A floral rosette (or oval) is created with a running backstitch of the outlines and a lazy-stitch fill-in, then the perfectly round border is created. The remainder is filled in with the background color. Again, care must be taken not to stretch the hide out of shape.

When a rosette is not sewn down to another surface, but instead backed with hide, the traditional method is to sew the backing to the rosette using an edge beading technique. And it eliminates the need to sew it first and then bead it. The edge is finished with beadwork in much the same way a small pouch can be sewn up with just the edge beading method. This can be seen in the clever little Mohawk puzzle pouches.

PICTOGRAPHIC STYLES

Various combinations of lazy stitch, running or spot stitch, and appliqué are used to create a stylistic pictographic form of beadwork based on realistic depictions of exploits, courtship, hunting, or sacred motifs. As defined here, *realism* is a loose term, because color and realism are not important partners in pictographic beadwork, just as they are not in ledger drawings or painted buffalo robes. Green or pink elk, and red or blue horses, are frequent components of pictographic beadwork, taking on a whimsical value. Realism with color may be found in white-based, black-tipped feathers, for example, or in navy blue beads with a line of white to simulate blue trade cloth leggings on a warrior. But generally speaking, the use of color in pictographic design, except for contrast, is not nearly as important as the meaning of the work, or the symbolism behind it.

Historically, all geometric work—painting on hide or parfleche, beadwork, and quillwork—was done by women, and representational or realistic painting was done by men, especially among many Plains nations. Since beadwork was not done by men, the realistic designs were sketched on the hide—a pipe bag or a possible bag are two examples—and the women beaded the pattern using their experience to choose the colors and other subtle interpretations. Thus, pictographic beadwork represented a collaborative effort between men and women.

As in painted or drawn pictographic forms, realistic beadwork always occurred with the action facing or proceeding to the *left* side of the work as it was viewed. (The only exceptions to this were beaded vests or coats upon which the representational figures, horses, or animals faced into the garment's front opening.) On two-sided pipe bags, the action similarly faced left and continued around to the back side of the bag so that a complete circle was formed coming around to the front again. Often it included slight overlaps, such as a horse's leg or the bottom corner of a tipi. This style is typical of some Cheyenne River Sioux work from before the turn of the century.

Rarely was the buffalo depicted realistically in painted forms, except in some Shoshone and Arapaho robes, and almost never in beadwork. There were some curvilinear buffalo motifs used, such as an elliptical oval with tapered, curved horns. Most pictographic beadwork illustrated dramatic exploits or military adventures—mounted warriors coming down on standing figures, with clearly different hairstyles or other obvious tribal distinctions. During the period called by some the western Indian Wars, it was common to see depictions of American flags, often with the colors reversed and only several stars or stripes. The purpose was not to copy exactly, either in color or form, but to represent, and no one could fail to recognize the symbolic American flag, no matter how distorted it appeared. Likewise, the five-pointed star, such as that seen on military epaulets, was adopted as a symbol of power in beadwork.

Other forms of pictographic beadwork, similar to ancient petroglyphs, are made up with lines, squares, diagonals, and triangles, and are composed to create bird, horse, deer, elk, or other animal motifs. Referred to by some as "thunderbirds," they are often found on the toes, or "flying" in the borders around the soles of moccasins, particularly on Northern Plains styles. Similarly, around the borders of moccasins can be found deer or horse motifs, with the center of the moccasins made up with the typical "buffalo track" design. These are geometric patterns with no curvilinear makeup, except of course for the natural shape of the moccasin, which forces the rows to curve around the toe, with the pattern of squares and diagonals contained within the row. These individual motifs—deer, horses, or thunderbirds—are always one-color patterns, usually red or dark blue on a white background of solid beadwork.

Pictographic beadwork is also the ideal place and format to use mixed bead colors—meaning that all beadworkers have accidents from time to time, and neat, separate piles of beads can spill or inadvertently become mixed. Rather than spending hours sorting thousands of seed beads back into separate color piles, they can be used for the creation of spotted-paint ponies, starry-sky nights, and backgrounds, to name a few, with dazzling effects.

Generally speaking, pictographic work is for the more advanced beadworker whose experience includes all the beading techniques. This style relies more on design than technique, but technique is necessary to create the finished work, and requires more competence.

It should be noted that within the field of pictorial beadwork, many sources supply "patterns" purported to be Native American—hummingbirds, bucking broncos, shooting stars, etc. These patterns are not Native and are best left to craftworkers and needlepointers; they have no business in traditional Native beadwork.

══ On COLOR and PATTERN ══

It cannot be emphasized enough how important the use of color is in the creation of traditional beadwork, and the relationship that color plays on itself. Successful beadworkers realize how colors affect the overall work, and are careful that no color becomes lost. Every color is meant to integrate yet stand apart and show up, even at considerable distance.

Crow beadwork is an outstanding example of broad areas of color, often done on red or blue wool with open spaces of fabric, and single lines of white beadwork separating individual design elements such as hourglass and diamond shapes. Crow beadwork

also employs the "softer" pale colors—pinks, yellows, and sky blues—using the harder, brighter wool backgrounds to bring out these colors.

This is also a consideration in eastern-style beadwork, where red or blue wool is used to bring out the boldness of white-only beadwork. Quite often navy, maroon, and purple velvets serve as a soft background, absorbing the light and making the beadwork jump off the piece. Thus, the background or surface color is also important, not just the relationship of the bead colors—especially from a creative point of view.

The background color of the beads

in broad area beadwork has a great effect on the design element colors. Lakota and Cheyenne work is dominated by white backgrounds and seconded with a medium blue, often with a slight lavender tint to it. The main design colors are in striking contrast: dark blue and dark green with borders of red, interior elements of light blue and yellow, and all arranged so that no color borders one of a similar hue or tone, thus creating the kind of contrast that makes each color stand out. Of course, reverse arrangements are common—navy blue borders, green interiors with red or yellow hearts. In essence, the contrasting colors are opposites on the color wheel.

Different colors and contrasts are often employed as backgrounds by various nations. Some fully beaded Blackfoot dress yokes are solid navy blue with geometrics of lighter contrasting colors—light blues, greens, yellows, and reds. Arapaho cradle boards are often solid yellow with diagonal stripes of red, blue, and white. Kiowa and Comanche often use dark colors like navy and green mixed with painted fringe in their moccasin borders and rows up high-top, fringed women's boots. And white as the contrast always stands out against dark backgrounds.

However, all rules are often broken, and unusual color combinations and patterns abound. The point is, just as all art is subjective, so is beadwork, and the dividing line between good and poor beadwork (not count-ing technique) is the use of color, pattern, and contrast. This is not something a beadworker can learn overnight, and it requires years of experience and exposure to other beadworkers and their products to fully know all the nuances separating average work from outstanding pieces. Anyone dedicated to beadwork will pour through books, visit museums and galleries showing older work, study the development, and set in his or her mind color combinations and patterns.

Comparing beadwork to parfleche will also reveal certain tribal distinctions, and also demystify the process of building a pattern. Parfleche (from the French *parer la flèche*, "to ward off an arrow," and named for rawhide shields) is a group of rawhide containers—boxes and trunks, cylindrical fringed cases, flat envelope-style wall pockets, and folded, flat meat cases—that are are brightly painted with geometric designs, generally leaving significant areas of white rawhide exposed, like beadwork on a white field. Crow parfleche designs with double hourglass and diamond centers are very similar to Crow beadwork; Lakota parfleche, with more intricate designs of squares and triangles, and outlines of blue or black lines, frequently resembles Lakota beadwork; Cheyenne parfleche, with fine lines extending from squares, often matches Cheyenne bead patterns, etc. Similarly, Apache rawhide with cutout diamonds, sawtooth edges, and backed with red wool on saddlebags takes on similar properties of some Apache beadwork. Thus, though not always the case, tribal design distinctions overlap media, such that familiarization with one art form within a tribal group often leads to a better understanding of several art forms within a broad context.

An interesting approach to beadwork is to bead the same piece or design several times, but with different color combinations. For instance, an overall pattern with a white background may be duplicated with a medium-blue background to create an entirely different effect, especially the way colors relate to each other. Or reversing the contrasting color on the same background will produce strikingly different results. Experiment with different hues of the same color.

One tricky problem is that of symbolism in beadwork, which frustrates Native Americans and anthropologists alike. Anthropologists seem to think that every beadwork design within every tribe must stand for or represent something, despite many Native claims that the pattern is merely esthetically pleasing. The real truth is that many patterns have names based on what they resemble in life or nature, but the work is not necessarily a tribute to that identity. Crosses, morning stars, tipis, mountains, horse tracks, caterpillars, whirlwinds, dragonflies, rain, thunder, lightning—all are some common terms that describe universally recognized symbols, but in combination with other design elements they may

be purely decorative. This is not to say that beadworkers never create designs with specific meanings, personal or otherwise, but it is best not to ascribe a symbolic meaning to beadwork other than one's own. Certainly, pictographic designs carry meaning, but often the exact meaning is personal—although the general meaning, such as a military exploit or a courtship scene, is clearly identifiable.

Often the symbolism lies within the object itself or its intended use, and the beadwork is a glorification, a respectful beautification, of the object. An example may be a sealed container in a turtle, lizard, or dragonfly shape that holds an infant's umbilical cord—a tradition among Plains nations—which connects the child to his mother and serves to protect his or her life during the first fragile years. The beadwork may or may not be symbolic as well, but the power is invested in the object and what it represents. Similarly, other objects intended to protect or carry sacred items, such as a pipe bag, may or may not have sacred beading on them, but the very nature of symbolism is personal.

Within this category may fall fully beaded moccasins, including the soles. These types of moccasins, normally with hard rawhide soles, must have soles of soft buckskin in order to be beaded, which precludes them from being worn by the living. These are moccasins for the dead, and it is known that during times like this, when communities and families came together to prepare for a funeral, some women went into a trancelike state and beaded for several days without sleep or rest to honor the departed. Other items were similarly beaded for the departed on their journey, when they crossed over. Objects like moccasins with fully beaded soles, or those that have absolutely no sign of use or wear, are often stolen from burial sites. (Note also that many people who were forced onto reservations often made beadwork to survive, trading or selling it to the wives of Indian agents, doctors, or military personnel, who collected it on shelves—hence, no wear.)

The concern with symbolism besides pattern and color must also include numbers. Certain nations regard numbers as important, such that repetitive sequences of design motifs like crosses or tracks may be significant to the maker or user of the object. Again, generalizations are dangerous with any form of personal artistic expression. Four is a special number among many nations, and so is seven and twelve, each having to do with direc-tions or spirits or prayers, but it is not likely that number arrangements in beadwork can be identified with absolute clarity, nor is it necessary that they should be. The number three is significant among Mohawk people, but is not a strong presence in beadwork.

Similarly the color white may represent the north, blue the west, green or yellow the south, and red the east, but it cannot be inferred (as almost always happens) that the use of these colors is significant of the four directions. What is more often a signifier of a sacred object, or any object of special meaning or purpose, is the use of red earth paint (ochre) or red powdered trade paint rubbed into the exposed leather or fringes. Other colors of paint may also represent personal beliefs, but the exact meaning belongs to the person. It should also be understood that beadwork of a personal nature was often contracted to an artist of exceptional ability who was only instructed as to what designs and colors to use, but with no knowledge of what they represented.

Other Applications

Among the Crow and other nations, beadwork on rawhide was fairly common, especially for knife cases. However, rawhide cannot be sewn with a lazy stitch, which passes just under the surface, so the sewing, always done with sinew, passed completely through the thin rawhide and crisscrossed on the back surface. The rawhide was then folded or backed to cover and protect the stitches. On knife cases only the broad outer edge was beaded and the inside of the case was smooth rawhide. Often a flap in an hourglass shape extended up and over the top of the case to keep the knife from fall-

ing out, and its edge was beaded with a tight, rolled edging technique.

For other rawhide objects, such as flat cases (sometimes called *wall pockets*), beadwork was done on strips, circles, or wedges of hide and then stitched separately onto the rawhide. Other objects like war bonnets had beadwork applied on separate strips across the brow, and triangular-shaped tabs, forked wedges, or squares were often appended from the handles of tomahawks, war clubs, dance wands, or the bottom corners of tipi bags or possible bags. (The term *possible* comes from the idea that the bag could contain anything possible—a catchall for anything from clothing to tools.)

In the same way that a round awl case or handle is beaded, a simple thong is also beaded, usually to hang in matched pairs from the bottom point of a knife case. The pattern is a series of bands or lines of color. The same thong beading technique is also used to create increasingly longer loops that become an old-style necklace. Thong beading, whether all around or with edge stitches, is best accomplished by stretching the thong between two points, such as at the ends of a bow to create tension.

Though not a beadwork technique in the sense that beads are sewn to hide, it is worth mentioning a method of running or stringing beads up yarns, which are then finger-woven into wide sashes with a bright pattern of beads (most often white) or braided for fringe, especially among Great Lakes and Northeast Woodland art. This technique is often employed to enhance the weaving patterns of sashes, knee garters, and shoulder bags.

= A Final Note About Color =

If there is any one color the bead-worker should respect, it is white. From solid backgrounds to edge work, outlines or thongs, white beads demand attention and bring the work to life. There is not a tribal style of beadwork that does not employ white beads, and their use outnumbers every other color. It is not so much that they were more common in the early days or that they are less expensive to produce, but that they stand in such stark, bright opposition to all other colors, or the color of hide or fabric. As hide darkens and other colors begin to recede into the background, white remains crisp. Even when corrupted by dirt and dust, white beadwork stands out. From Iroquois lace style to Crow line work, from Lakota backgrounds to Kiowa details within navy rows, white beads always define the patterns. They accentuate the rich scarlet and navy trade cloths; they become like a field of snow for sharp geometric patterns. When they outline floral work in free form against aged hide, the colors of the other beads blossom.

The traditional beadworker will often use twice as many whites as any other color.

Glossary

Antler versus horn: Antler is a bone-like growth from the skulls of deer, elk, moose, caribou, etc. which drop off and are replaced each year, nourished by a covering of blood vessels referred to as *velvet*. Antlers have points or projections called *tines* growing off a main beam. The main beams are used for the handles of hide-scraping tools, and the tines often for awl or quirt handles. Horns, which are found on buffalo, sheep, antelope, and domestic cattle, are actually a hair-like growth over a curved bone projection from the skull. Horns do not drop off, and when removed from the bone core are hollow. Horns are often used for spoons, bows (archery), and combs. The term "deer horn" is incorrect.

Awl: Awl blades were a popular trade item and were set in antler, bone, or wood handles. They are called blades because—unlike modern round awls—they were triangular or diamond shaped, which allowed them to cut or slice through the hide cleanly and easily. Larger holes, for instance in rawhide or parfleches, were more often burned with a red-hot wire or the heated head of a nail.

Brain-tanned: Leather (moose, deer, elk, antelope, buffalo, caribou, or any furbearing skin) that is non-chemically tanned and softened using the animal's brains in a natural process. The term *brain-tanned* has become a universal designation for Native leather although some processes use fish or bear oil, or other natural ingredients.

Brass tacks: Often used on beaded objects, such as Crow rawhide knife cases, the old brass tacks have a square brass nail shank and a domed hollow head. Modern brass tacks have a round steel nail shank. These tacks are also used in belts and pouches of harness leather. Other objects adorned with tacks include antler scraper tools, "Gunstock-style" war clubs, pipestems, wooden quirt handles, and the wooden frames of cradleboards.

Crow bead: A necklace-size bead of solid color which can be strung on a thong.

Dew claws: Dew claws, and the toes of deer, elk, and buffalo are similar to horn in that they grow around bone and are hollow. Used for rattles and decoration on clothing and bandolier straps.

Parfleche: Rawhide that is whitened and painted in geometric designs. It is used for meat cases (envelopes), boxes or trunks, wall pockets (flat cases that hang from the lining in tipis), cylindrical fringed containers for bonnets or medicine, mortars for pounding cherries, knife cases, sun shades, etc. All painting is done on the "flesh" side—the hair side is too smooth and non-porous for paint. Traditionally, parfleche is painted on the wet "green" hide and the hair pounded off. This whitens the hide and makes it flexible. It is said that the term parfleche comes from the combination of the French *parer*—to ward off or deflect—and *fleche*—arrow—which described the rawhide shields which could turn away arrows in battle.

Pony bead: Any bead of size 8/0 or larger, so called because beads were shipped in packs on horses to hard to reach mountain and plateau regions. The most prominent colors were white, light blue, black, and red. An early style beadwork among upper Missouri River nations, these beads continued on later in Blackfoot, Nez Percé, Shoshone, and Bannock (as well as others) dresses and articles of clothing.

Rawhide: An animal hide (such as deer, elk, moose, or buffalo) that is untreated with chemicals or brains, dehaired, stretched, and dried, and which becomes hard and shiny like a drum head or moccasin soles. Rawhide shrinks as it dries and is used to wrap metal blades on scraper tools, club handles, etc. The color is generally amber or yellow, though when pounded it becomes whitened. Rawhide is also used for webbing on snowshoes, lacrosse sticks, etc.

Seed bead: Any of the small colored beads which fall between size 18/0 to 10/0, the latter being the larger size.

Sequins: A small loop of brass or silver flattened with a stamping machine to produce a disk with a hole in the center. Sequins are often sewn on breechcloths or other clothing and bags in decorative patterns.

Sinew: A silvery grey tendon which travels down each side of the spine on mammals. It is scraped free of all flesh and allowed to dry, then shredded into fibers which are moistened and twisted into sewing threads.

Sizing: A coating of hide glue—made from the boiled scrapings of rawhide—that protects and seals the painted designs on parfleche, robes, or articles of clothing. Powdered trade paints were also mixed in hide glue.

Smoke-tanned: Not a tanning process but a final process used *after* brain tanning or oil tanning in which the naturally processed hide is smoked for hours to color it any of a range of shades of brown, from honey to almost chocolate. A common misconception is that smoked hide is waterproof. It is not. The smoking process impregnates the hide with natural resins that make it less susceptible to water damage when new. Generally a process which spread south from snowy regions during the twentieth century. There are few old pieces below the Canadian border that are smoked.

Tin cones: Originally cut from tin cans (technically they should be called "tinned cans," because the sheet metal was layered with tin to prevent rusting), these small cones hung from the fringes of beaded pouches, clothing, knife cases, moccasins, etc. They produce a pleasant jingling sound. The old handmade tin cones have a much more exaggerated flair than the modern, straighter, machine-made version.

Trade bead: A necklace-size bead usually of multicolors, common in trade, and often found hung from thongs on clothing or ceremonial regalia.

Trade cloth: Also called *stroud* or *baize*, trade cloth is woven of white wool yarns then dipped in dye with the selvage edge clamped between boards (which often have a sawtooth pattern cut in the edge); the resulting scarlet, navy blue, green, or black fabric exhibits a white, undyed edge, often with the above mentioned sawtooth pattern. Late nineteenth century and twentieth century trade cloth is yarn dyed before weaving and often has colored yarns along the two outside selvage edges, hence the term "rainbow cloth."

Trade paint: Originally all pigmentation of hides, fringes, parfleche, etc. was done with earth ochres in various shades of red, brown, yellow, pale green, blue, and black. Europeans brought and traded bright powdered pigments which were mixed with water or hide glue, or dry brushed into the fibers of the leather or cloth. Today, powdered tempera or poster paints perform exactly the same task as trade paints.

White-heart: A bead, either in seed or necklace size, which is composed of an opaque white core with an outer wrapping of translucent colored glass, most often red. Yellow and light blue are also common. The old red style is a soft rose color, often referred to as "rose-white-lined."

APPENDIX 1
Beading Before and After Construction

As a guide for new beadworkers, it is important to define those objects that are beaded before or after construction, objects that have applied beadwork or that are perhaps wrapped with hide and then beaded. Careful study of the traditional items in the color photographs will help to clarify.

Beaded Before Construction. All hard-sole (rawhide) moccasin uppers (be sure to leave ¼ inch seam allowance); round, oval, or square fringed pouches (pouches are assembled later and then the fringing is cut—otherwise it will be a nuisance with your beading thread); possible bags are optional (some find it easier to bead before, some after, but the seams are obviously beaded after construction); pipe bags are beaded after the side seam is sewn but before the quillwork and fringing is added; shirt strips, legging strips, and blanket bands, which are added to garments; rosettes; cradle board covers; dresses; wool appliqués (such as those found on moccasin toe vamps, rifle scabbards, and shoulder bags); knife cases; tabs and hangings from handles, such as quirts, war clubs, etc.; thongs; brow bands; gaunlets and wrist cuffs; women's leggings; amulets (except umbilical cases); armbands; most eastern and Great Lakes bandolier-style bag panels and other eastern woolen objects; northwest and Alaskan wool objects, such as octopus bags; added-on moccasin flaps (such as Winnebago, Iroquois, Sac and Fox, and Pottowatomie).

Beaded After Construction. Front-seam moccasins; all seams on bags, dresses, strike-a-light pouches; awl cases; umbilical cases; amulets; fan handles; quivers and bow cases; free-design work on garments such as vests, jackets, or dresses; floral work on bags or pouches; tops of bags, pouches, quivers, knife cases; dolls; stuffed-hide shinny balls; rifle cases without wool.

Wrapped and Beaded. Numerous round objects are wrapped or encased in hide, then beaded with peyote stitch, lazy stitch, or running back-stitch. Among them are feathers, drumsticks, whistles, club handles, gourd rattles, dance wands or sticks, awl handles (rare), and round tobacco bundles.

APPENDIX 2
Native American Hide Tanning

The original and best way to take care of a hide is to immediately remove all the fat, flesh, blood, and membranes on the inside. Stretch it in a frame of wood or stake it to the ground (hair side down) and let the air and sun dry it quickly. Bacteria cannot grow in a bone-dry environment, and a hide treated like this will be stable for years—it is rawhide, like a drumhead. (It should be noted that one product on the market for years, a hide that everyone calls "rawhide laces" for boots, etc., is not rawhide at all but commercially oil-tanned bull hide. Rawhide is hard as nails and tougher to cut than some sheet metal!) A hide should be stretched in all directions and made as tight as possible. Another method is to nail the hide to the side of a barn or wooden shed where it will quickly dry in the sun. Be warned—a larger hide such as cow, moose, or buffalo will shrink considerably, bending the nails inward, and in some cases it has actually torn the boards from the side of the barn.

Regardless, the most important thing is to get the hide stretched tight and bone dry, and it must be completely free of fat, flesh, and membranes.

There are several ways to accomplish this: (1) The hide can be fleshed with a curved fleshing knife while stretched on the ground or in a wooden frame. The knife must make even, curved cuts to remove everything from the skin. (2) A toothed, sharp flesher, made originally from an old gun barrel, digs at the flesh, picks it up, and tears it off. And (3) the hide is draped over a fleshing beam and a double-handled fleshing knife slices away the meat and fat (Figure 25). All three methods work well, and also force some internal oils and moisture out of the hide, enabling it to dry more quickly.

When the hide is completely dry, the sharp scraper tool is used to pare away the thin membranes that still remain on the flesh side. On buffalo and large animals, there is a layer not easily detected when the hide is fleshed that is composed of fine cross-hatching sinews or nerves. These are the forces that allow the animal to "twitch" off flies and insects in the field, but they also prevent the braining solution or tanning oils from penetrating the hide. On buffalo, they are especially tough, and require hard work to scrape off. At the same time,

FIGURE 24 · WORKING WITH HIDE

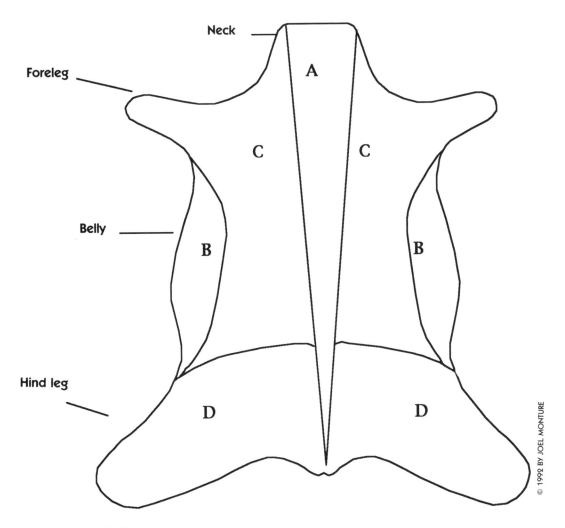

Neck

Foreleg

A

C   C

Belly

B   B

Hind leg

D   D

© 1992 BY JOEL MONTURE

A. This is the neck and spine section, which is generally thicker and tougher. Good for soft-sole moccasins.

B. The belly/underarm portion that stretches in all directions. Not good for sturdier projects; very thin.

C. The general-usage section—shoulders and sides.

D. Considered by many the best part of a hide, the hips or flanks, which are not too thick and very dense.

FIGURE 25 · THE "BREAKING BEAM"

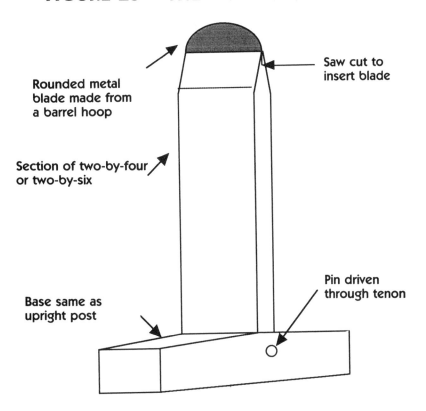

Saw cut to insert blade

Rounded metal blade made from a barrel hoop

Section of two-by-four or two-by-six

Base same as upright post

Pin driven through tenon

Pull hide back and forth over beam

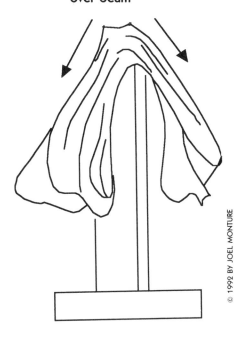

© 1992 BY JOEL MONTURE

it is advisable to pare down the thicker portions of the hide—the neck and spine, and the hips, which are very dense with membranes.

The hide is then turned over (either the frame is reversed or it is unstaked from the ground and restaked), and the hair is removed along with the upper layer of epidermis, using the same antler scraper tool. It is best to work from the neck down, creating an open area along the spine, and then working to the right and left of the hide out to the edges and legs. Even though it is rawhide, there is some elasticity to the hide, and it is hard to break through unless the corners of the scraper are sharp, dig in, and slice right through. Use a file to knock off any sharp corners on the tool. If the hide was dried on a barn wall, take it down and place it on the ground, but over an old carpet or tarp to prevent dirt and grass from staining it as you apply pressure from above. The hair must be removed down to the follicle; otherwise there will be a "stubble."

It should now be a perfect "brainable" rawhide, almost white, and ready to accept moisture. The hide is now soaked in clear water or in a stream/ lake until it is completely relaxed—it can then be pulled and stretched in all directions. Next wring it out, making it as dry as possible.

The preparation of the brains vary from nation to nation. In Alaska, an Athapascan method puts *rotten* brains in a cloth sack and lets them simmer in warm water until the water turns milky white with brain oil. The brains are discarded and only the "brain water" is used to soak the hide. A Plains method is to cook up the brains then mash them into the raw skin with a stone. The absolute point is to get the oils into the hide, but nowhere are brains used raw—always cooked, no matter how slightly. Sometimes a hide was used for rawhide, not tanned, and the brains were cooked up with moss and molded into thin cakes that were sun-dried for later use. A current method is to cook up brains with three parts water until they are gray/white and an iridescent froth has formed on the water, just like soap bubbles. When the brains and water have cooled, put them in a blender until they are pureed into a smooth batter. The damp, raw hide is then put into a large tub and the brains poured over the hide. All the brains are hand-rubbed and kneaded into the hide. Every square inch on both sides is coated, and the hide is squeezed until the brains literally bubble and hiss through the porous skin. This means that all the hide fibers are soaked in brains. The hide can be worked soon, but some prefer to wrap it up in a plastic bag and let it "sweat" overnight in a cool place. Be warned—the smell of brains is unpleasant if you're not used to it, and if brains start to go bad, the hide should be washed off immediately in buckets of clear water. It should not have to be "rebrained." Some inexperienced people say you should brain the hide six to ten times, but one good deep braining works perfectly, provided the hide was properly fleshed and scraped, and dehaired with all the upper scarf skin to create porous surfaces.

The brains may come from the animal itself or they may be from calf or pork. The type of brains does not matter. Other methods were used, and lacking brains, willow bark, red clay, fish or bear oil, or soap tanning is a substitute. A strong mixture of Ivory soap flakes in water, or Murphy's oil soap, works very well to get the tanner to the next step.

The idea behind the next step is simple—the moisture in the hide has to be removed completely, and the fibers have to be flexible. This is what a finished hide is like, dry and soft.

A hide that is drying without motion or movement will shrink, harden, and eventually become rawhide.

There are two ways to accomplish the drying and softening. One way is to wring the hide very completely, such as wrapping it around a sapling in a twisted loop and using a stick to turn the hide—kind of like winding up a rubber band—until all the moisture has dripped out of the skin. Brains and oils will also drip away, but that's all right. The second method is to lace the hide in a frame again, as tight as possible, and in essence "squeegee" the water out of it with a wide, dull metal blade or paddle.

The second method is advantageous because the hide is overstretched beyond its skinned-out size, and thinner, which makes it a large

hide, ideal for clothing. The first method, with no frame stretching, allows the hide to shrink in a little—making it thicker, which is good for eastern or soft-soled moccasins.

The framing method stretches the fibers out as the water is scraped away, and the continuous motion keeps them soft and flexible.

The wringing method requires hideworkers to continually stretch the hide in all directions to keep the fibers moving and soft as the hide continues to evaporate away the remaining moisture. It is common for several people to sit or stand and "pull" the hide, first from neck to tail, then from belly to belly, then from right front leg to left hind leg on the diagonal—in short, *every* direction and every square inch is continuously stretched and worked, creating a friction that speeds up the drying. The same thing is accomplished by "paddling" the hide in the frame, stretching the fibers with a tool as the moisture is drawn down the hide to drip on the floor or ground.

When the hide feels as dry as it's going to get, it's not. There is always some moisture left in it that will allow the hide to shrink back and become stiffer. At this time, the hide is "roped." A rope or cord needs to be solidly fixed between two points—from ceiling to floor, barn beam to barn post, or tree limb to tree trunk—so that the hide can be brought around the rope and pulled back and forth with sufficient speed and friction to soften and dry it completely. This process also fluffs up the hide and makes it ideal for beadwork. (One note: If there are any holes in the hide, the time to sew them up is just before the hide is roped. The roping will fluff up the fibers enough to almost cover the stitches and smooth out most of the distortion created by bringing the edges of the holes together.)

Invariably there will be edges or spots that stiffen up and turn yellow (remember that *all* hide is white when done, even commercial skins, but they are dyed to look like the stereotypical "buckskin"). A pair of pliers can be used to grip edges and pull the hide fibers soft, working all along the edges to get the extra inch or so of hide softened. Another method for softening edges or spots in the interior of a hide is the use of a breaking beam, which is either a vertical piece of wood on a stand with a tapered edge or a piece of iron barrel hoop inserted as a softening edge. The hide is briskly rubbed back and forth over the edge, breaking down the fibers (Figure 26).

Modern technology provides an interesting twist on an old method, and a possible benefit. If for any reason the drying/softening process must be interrupted or put on hold, the hide(s) can be frozen in plastic bags. The expansion of frozen ice crystals within the fibers opens up the hide and acts to keep them apart. Freezing is also an indication of how much moisture exists within a particular hide. An example would be a soaking-wet T-shirt put in the freezer. It would be impossible to simply open it up upon re-moval—until it thawed. Similarly, a hide without moisture content cannot freeze, and will come out of the freezer soft and limp.

Lastly, smoking the hide is the final option. Hide-smoking is accomplished by the simple and continuous action of smoke against leather. Generally, a pit is dug and a bed of coals created with a hot fire over which punky or rotten wood is placed—sometimes mosses or rotten bark, which smolder billows of smoke into a hide that has been sewn into a bag over the pit. The hide is inverted so that both sides are smoked, and usually the hair side is allowed to smoke a little darker. There is a chance the smoldering materials will flare up, and any real heat or fire will destroy the leather. *No* fire should ever be present, *only smoke*! One way to accomplish this and safeguard the hide is to have the fire and the hide in different places. A two-foot length of stovepipe with an elbow section facing down over the smoke pit, and an elbow section facing up into the hide bag two feet away, will ensure that only smoke wafts up into the leather, and if fire does erupt from the pit, the hide is sufficiently protected. Smoked hide should be rolled up for a week or two to let the oily resins "settle" in. Some of the simplest smoking occurred just by hanging up the hides in the path of smoke in the tipi or longhouse.

In fact, all brain-tanned hide should be rolled, and never folded, because folding creates creases that sometimes set in the leather after a period of stor-

FIGURE 26 · ROPING A HIDE

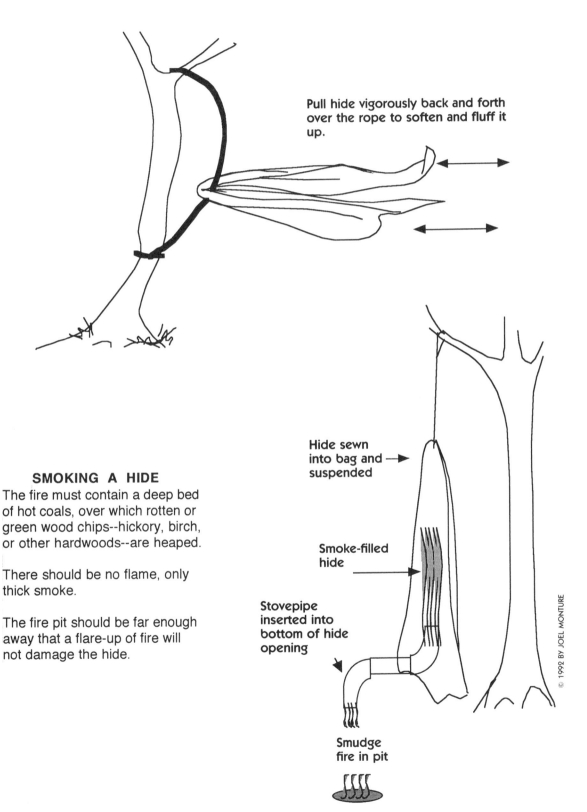

Pull hide vigorously back and forth over the rope to soften and fluff it up.

Hide sewn into bag and → suspended

Smoke-filled hide

Stovepipe inserted into bottom of hide opening

Smudge fire in pit

SMOKING A HIDE

The fire must contain a deep bed of hot coals, over which rotten or green wood chips--hickory, birch, or other hardwoods--are heaped.

There should be no flame, only thick smoke.

The fire pit should be far enough away that a flare-up of fire will not damage the hide.

© 1992 BY JOEL MONTURE

age. Creases make it difficult to lay a hide out flat and create patterns, and the creases may later "relax" after the beadwork is done.

HIDEWORKING TOOLS A good set of hideworking tools will last a lifetime and can be passed on to others who will continue to use them with respect. It is sad to see such tools lying dormant in museum displays, the tools a woman used to clothe her children (for women originally were the hideworkers). The old tools sing out to be used again. If you cannot use old tools, however, you must make new ones, and they should be made properly.

An elk antler scraper is an essential tool. It is as if the Creator intended only one use for that part of an elk antler, because nothing in nature—no branch or bone—ever seems so uniform, so suited for that particular purpose. But elk antler is somewhat ridged and coarse, and all the old tools are so beautifully smooth and polished, the patina even further enhanced by the thousands of hours of hand-rubbing while in use.

The antlers were cut and shaped uniformly. There was a centuries-old notion of exactly what the tools had to be, because the same tool, made in different decades by different nations, has almost the exact same angle, length, and surface finish. This was not a tool that changed with time because it needed no improvements.

The basic hide scraper was made from the main beam at the second tine of an elk antler; it was laboriously rasped, filed, or scraped to a mirror-smooth finish, and fitted with an iron or steel blade secured in place with shrunken rawhide thong wrappings. It was and is a beautiful object, both in form and function (Figure 27).

The blade should be made from hardened steel, and the best source now, as then, is a section of saw blade. The old two-man lumber saws are great for scraper blades because they hold a good sharp edge even when paring down rawhide. The cutting edge should not be straight across, but only slightly curved to the corners. Some people make the edge a half-moon shape, but this concentrates the cuts in a small line, which produces uneven ridges on the finished hide. The corners of the blade should be rounded off so they do not score or cut through the hide (Figure 28). Lastly, the bevel of the blade should be at an extreme angle, like a knife, making it easier to sharpen. This extreme bevel allows the blade to cut deeper and pare off the hide or hair like curled woodshavings from a block plane (Figures 29–34).

Fleshers were originally made from the femur (major hind-leg bone) of large mammals including buffalo, moose, bear, and deer, but in later years shotgun barrels or steel pipes were used. A section of metal 12 to 16 inches was used, as it essentially imitated a leg bone. One end is heated red hot and flattened with a hammer on a stone or anvil, which spreads the cylinder apart. The resulting curved

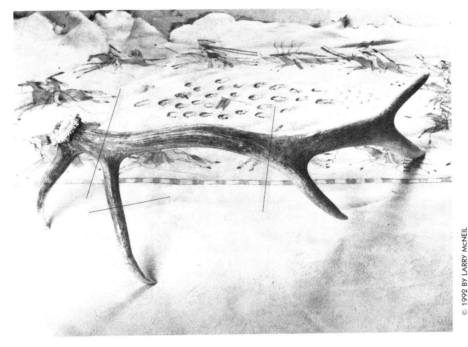

© 1992 BY LARRY McNEIL

FIGURE 27 · An elk antler, which has been used for countless generations to make the basic hideworking tool. The lines show the cuts that remove the excess material, leaving only the adz-like handle, which still needs to be shaped, smoothed, and polished.

edge is filed to a sharp bevel. A series of teeth are filed in the edge, and the handle part of the tool is covered with a sewn layer of hide, sometimes with a wrist strap attached. Oftentimes the hide was rubbed with earth ochers or trade paint, usually green or red.

There are two kinds of knives one needs to work with. The first has a very curved blade for fleshing the hide; the second is quite fine and pointed to pierce holes for lacing or staking the hide. Modern knives don't seem to have much play in them, meaning that the blades are hard steel and unflexible. Choose old knives that are thin-bladed, and relax when you work with them. The metal should have a spring quality. The best knives can be found in garage sales and flea markets for a dollar, often old kitchen or butcher knives with riveted slab-wood handles. The shape of the blade can be modified on a grinding wheel to suit the purpose—fleshing or piercing.

Lastly, a wide-bladed metal or wooden tool, or a breaking beam, is useful for removing moisture and softening hard edges.

FRAMING OR LACING HIDES
Most people who work hides spend too much time putting them on the frames and taking them off. Usually, they think that a lace has to go through a hole in the edge of hide and around the supporting member of the

© 1992 BY LARRY McNEIL

FIGURE 28 · The elk antler is rasped and filed smooth to fit the hand of Pat White, an Oneida hideworker.

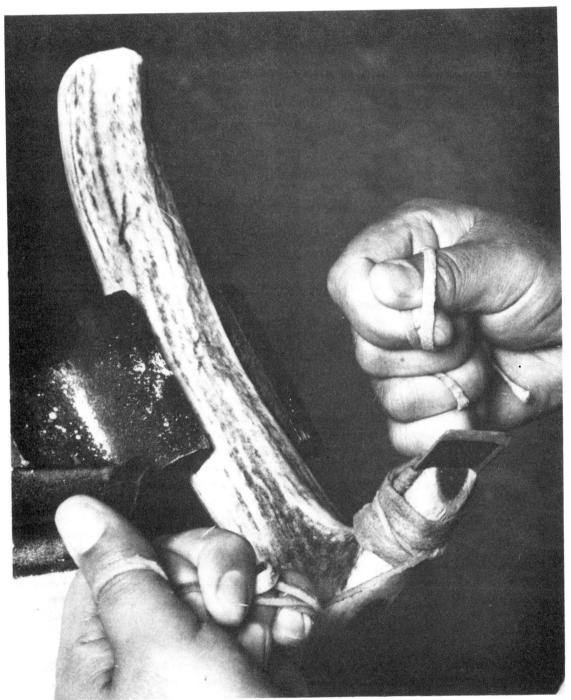

© 1992 BY LARRY McNEIL

FIGURE 29 · A piece of an old, thick saw blade has been cut and shaped with a sharp bevel. Then it is placed against the flat inside surface of the scraper handle and wrapped with wet rawhide by Colleen Flores, an Omaha hideworker. When the rawhide dries, the blade will be "locked" in place.

FIGURE 30 · IRON OR STEEL SCRAPER BLADE DESIGN

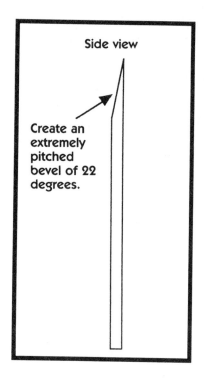

Side view

Create an extremely pitched bevel of 22 degrees.

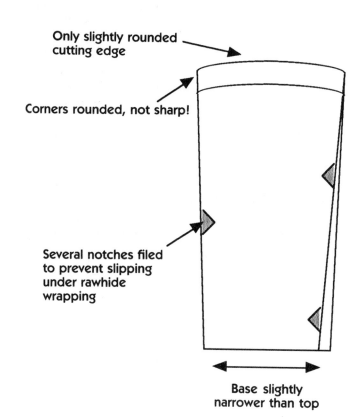

Only slightly rounded cutting edge

Corners rounded, not sharp!

Several notches filed to prevent slipping under rawhide wrapping

Base slightly narrower than top

ELK ANTLER SCRAPER SPECS

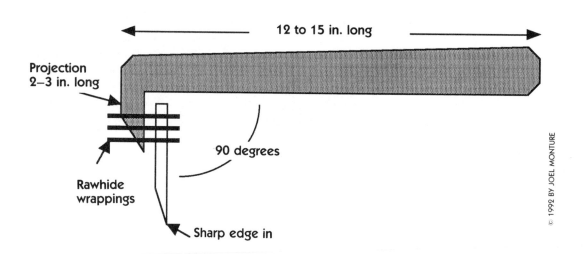

12 to 15 in. long

Projection 2–3 in. long

90 degrees

Rawhide wrappings

Sharp edge in

© 1992 BY JOEL MONTURE

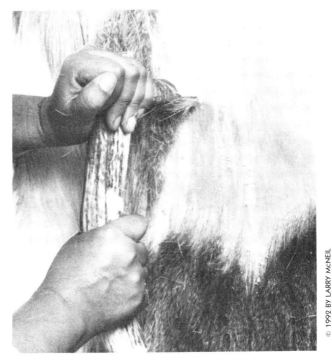

© 1992 BY LARRY McNEIL

FIGURE 31 · The blade is filed and honed very sharp, with care being taken to round off the corners so they don't dig in and score lines in the hide. Here Colleen Flores, an Omaha hideworker, uses the scraper to pare away the hair and upper epidermal layer of a whitetail deer hide that has been fleshed, stretched, and allowed to dry as hard as a drumhead.

© 1992 BY LARRY McNEIL

FIGURE 32 · *Left:* A Crow elk antler scraper, circa 1880. *Middle:* A Nez Percé elk antler scraper, circa 1870. *Right:* A Cheyenne elk antler scraper with brass tacks, circa 1875. Note how finished and polished the old tools are, with a smooth surface and a patina like ivory. (Author's collection.)

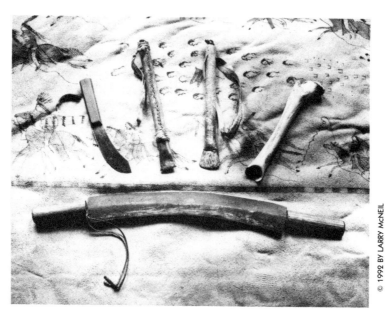

FIGURE 33 · Tools used to flesh hides. *Top, from left to right:* An English skinning/fleshing knife, circa 1880, of the type commonly traded in North America; two fleshing tools circa 1890, Lakota or Cheyenne, made from old gun barrels and wrapped with sinew-sewn hide; a femur bone flesher. *Bottom:* a two-handled, hand-forged fleshing knife, nineteenth century, used when hides are fleshed over a round beam or log. (Author's collection.)

FIGURE 34 · A paddle-bladed softening tool made from an old iron barrel hoop and a section of moose antler, used to squeeze the water and brains out of the hide, stretch and move the fibers, and rough up the surface. (Author's collection.)

FIGURE 35 · HIDE STRETCHING ON TWO-BY-FOUR FRAME

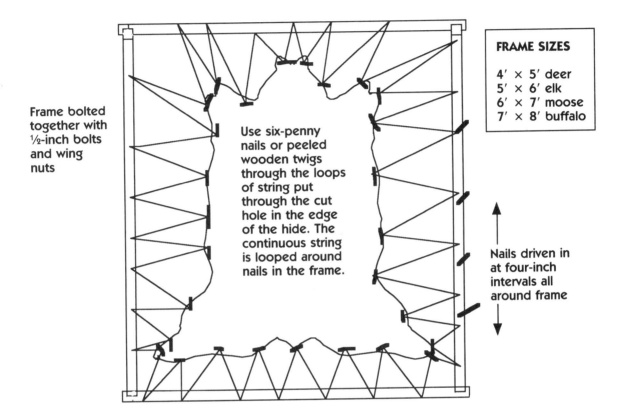

Frame bolted together with ½-inch bolts and wing nuts

Use six-penny nails or peeled wooden twigs through the loops of string put through the cut hole in the edge of the hide. The continuous string is looped around nails in the frame.

FRAME SIZES

4′ × 5′ deer
5′ × 6′ elk
6′ × 7′ moose
7′ × 8′ buffalo

Nails driven in at four-inch intervals all around frame

FIGURE 36 · DETAIL OF LACING

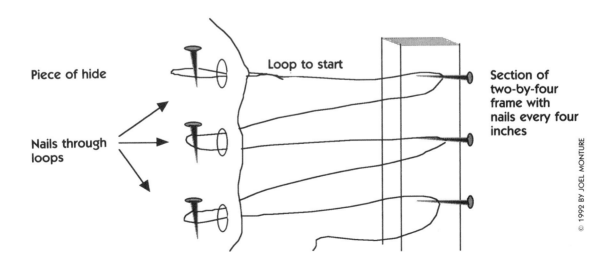

Piece of hide

Loop to start

Nails through loops

Section of two-by-four frame with nails every four inches

© 1992 BY JOEL MONTURE

frame. This will work, but sometimes a hide is large and has many small, loose edges that all have to be stretched tightly. The resulting effort is that a lace or string, perhaps fifty feet long or more, has to be pulled over and over again through dozens of holes around the perimeter of the hide to secure it within the frame (Figure 35).

This doesn't have to be so. An old way is to align the hide so that it hangs down from neck to tail (Figure 36). In the two corners of the neck, a hole is pierced with the framing knife. (A good frame is made out of bolted-together two-by-fours with six-penny nails driven in all around at three-inch intervals.) Hang the hide in the frame from the nails in the neck holes. Cut holes in each hind leg. Then use a piece of string/cord about two feet long tied with a loop at one end. Put the tip of the loop through the hole in the hind leg, and through the loop of string put a six-penny nail or a peeled twig. Repeat on the other hind leg, stretching both hind legs to their fullest and also drawing the length of the hide down its longest length. The hide

is now stretched at three points—neck, hind leg, hind leg.

Next, using short strings with tied loops, stretch out each foreleg. The hide will now resemble a tanned skin. Starting from the loose skin on either the right or left side, pierce a series of holes approximately every three or four inches along the outer edge, from the top of the neck down, and around to the tail. Repeat on the opposite side. Then, using string, peeled sticks, or nails, and starting from the top, begin to lace the hide into the frame, stretching it tightly. Tie the start of the cord to the topmost nail, bring it down, and loop it into the hole in the hide, placing a nail or stick through the loop of cord. Continue all around the hide, making sure it is stretched evenly. The benefit is that when the hide comes off the frame, it is only necessary to pull out the cord loop nails—one after another—rather than drawing fifty feet of cord through every single hole in the hide. The cord may then be undraped from the nails on the frame, coiled, and stored for use on the next hide.

Step-by-Step Brain Tanning Checklist

1. Rawhide fleshed clean of all meat, fat, and membranes.

2. Hide is stretched tightly in all directions in a frame or nailed to barn wall, then allowed to dry like a drumhead.

3. Hide is turned over and all the hair and upper layer of "scarf" skin is pared away with elk antler scraper tool. Membranes scraped off flesh side.

4. Hide is soaked in water until flexible in all directions, then wrung out.

5. Brains cooked in three parts water are blended and rubbed into both sides of hide, and hide is rolled up to "sweat" for several hours.

6. Hide is wrung out again and laced tightly into the frame again.

7. Paddle-edged metal tool scrapes both sides of hide, removing as much brains and moisture as possible, and keeping fibers moving. When hide is as dry as it can be at this stage, remove from frame.

8. Alternately pull the hide back and forth over a taut rope, and stretch the hide in all directions, continually keeping the fibers in motion as the last amounts of moisture evaporate. Use a metal-edged breaking post to soften hard edges.

9. If desired, when hide is completely finished, soft, and dry, sew it into a bag and smoke it with punky wood or hickory chips until it is a uniform brown color. Then roll it up and put it away for several weeks to "cure." (Be careful that only smoke, not heat or flames, comes near the hide.)

10. Remember to keep hides rolled, not folded, so permanent creases do not form.

APPENDIX 3
Sources

Beads, Needles, Wax, Basic Supplies:

Crazy Crow Trading Post
P.O. Box 314
Denison, TX 75020
(214) 463-1366

Elliot, Greene & Co.
37 West 37th Street
New York, NY 10018
(212) 391-9075

International Beadtrader
2750 South Broadway
Englewood, CO 80110
(303) 781-2657

Pierre Bovis Bead Co.
P.O. Box 460
220 E. Fremont Street
Tombstone, AZ 85638
(602) 457-3359

Wandering Bull, Inc.
247 South Main Street
Attleboro, MA 02703
(508) 226-6074

Western Trading Post, Inc.
32 Broadway
Denver, CO 80209
(303) 777-7750

Hides (Brain-Tanned and Smoked):

Eidness Hide and Fur
Rt. 4, Box 14
St. Maries, ID 83861
(208) 245-4753

Jim Bond, Ltd.
35113 Brewster Road
Lebanon, OR 97355
(503) 258-3645

Lietzau Taxidermy Co.
Box 12
Cosmos, MN 56228
(612) 877-7297 (raw and tanned buffalo, brain-tanned deer and moose)

Mark Humpal Leathers
RR 3, Box 39
Cornish, NH 03745
(603) 675-5350 (raw deer and
brain-tanned deer)

Matoska Trading Co.
P.O. Box 2004
Yorba Linda, CA 92686
(909) 393-0647

Suggested Reading

(*Note:* Although the publications from the Bureau of Indian Affairs are somewhat dated, they contain many patterns and photos of traditional art.)

Conn, Richard. *Circles of the World.* Denver: Denver Art Museum, 1982.

Ewers, John C. *Blackfeet Crafts.* Washington, D.C.: Department of the Interior, Bureau of Indian Affairs, 1945. (Currently in reprint.)

Ewers, John C. and William. *Crow Indian Beadwork.* Ogden, Utah: Eagle's View Publishing, 1985.

Lyford, Carrie A. *Iroquois Crafts.* Washington, D.C.: Department of the Interior, Bureau of Indian Affairs, 1945. (Currently in reprint.)

Lyford, Carrie A. *Quill and Beadwork of the Western Sioux.* Washington, D.C.: Department of the Interior, Bureau of Indian Affairs, 1940. (Currently in reprint.)

Thom, Laine. *Becoming Brave.* San Francisco: Chronicle Books, 1992.

Walters, Anna Lee. *The Spirit of Native America.* San Francisco: Chronicle Books, 1989.

BEADWORK PATTERN GRAPH

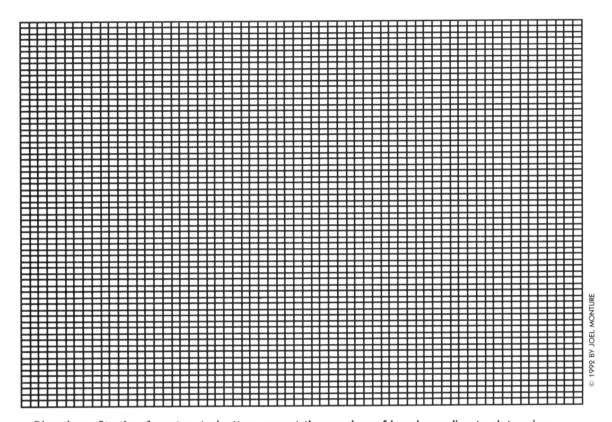

© 1992 BY JOEL MONTURE

Directions: Starting from top to bottom, count the number of beads per line to determine the width of the row. Draw a dark line to divide the rows. Fill in each bead square with a colored marker or pencil to build the pattern. Use this graph to record old-time patterns on old pieces for future reference.

INDEX

Numbers in italic refer to illustrations.